Guard Force
Management

Guard Force Management

Lucien G. Canton, CPP

Butterworth-Heinemann

Boston Oxford Melbourne Singapore Toronto
Munich New Delhi Tokyo

Library of Congress Cataloging-in-Publication Data
Canton, Lucien G.
    Guard force management / Lucien G. Canton.
       p. cm.
    Includes bibliographical references and index.
    ISBN 0-7506-9299-5 (hard : alk. paper)
      1. Private security services—United States—Management.
    2. Private security services—United States—Administration.
    I. Title.
    HV8291.U6C37 1995
    363.2'89'068—dc20   95-32405
                                                                          CIP

British Library Cataloguing-in-Publication Data
A catalogue record for this book is available from the British Library.

The publisher offers discounts on bulk orders of this book.
For information, please write:
Manager of Special Sales
Butterworth-Heinemann
313 Washington Street
Newton, MA 02158-1626

10 9 8 7 6 5 4 3 2 1

Printed in the United States of America

To my wife, Doreen, who believed I could do it, and to Richard and Katie, who grew up asking, "Aren't you done with that book yet, Dad?"

Contents

Preface

Several years ago, I was asked by a friend to survey available security texts and recommend a good basic text for his security officers' academy. At the time, I was forced to admit that the existing texts were not very useful for the purpose he had in mind. Thankfully, this situation has been remedied by a veritable explosion of excellent guard training texts published in the last few years.

In surveying available texts, I was struck by the fact that only one book had been published in recent years that addressed the training needs of the guard force manager. I thought back to my early days in the industry and how I desperately sought all the information I could get on my chosen profession. Many of the sources I used were outdated at the time and the only up-to-date information came from excerpts from general security textbooks. I was shocked that, given the incredible changes that have taken place in our industry over the past twenty years, these old texts and excerpts were still the only resources available to the novice guard force manager.

The last twenty years have seen our industry improve dramatically, becoming more professional and business-oriented—and increasingly more competitive. Survival in the guard business requires that a manager use all available tools to increase profit while providing quality service. The demands placed on managers by the increase in the use of computer technology, customer sophistication, and the threat of civil litigation require management that is focused, decisive, and attuned to modern management practices.

While writing this book I have continually asked myself the question, What would I have wanted to see in a management text when I was just starting out in the industry? I have also harbored the hope that some of the concepts in this book might change the thinking of those experienced managers who still feel that we can prosper by doing "business as usual" in this dynamic profession.

A brief note about the title—several colleagues have asked me why I chose to use the term "guard" rather than "security officer," particularly in view of my long-standing advocation of the latter title and its general acceptance in the industry. The answer is that the term "security officer" tends to be applied to the very best personnel the industry has to offer, with the term "guard" somehow denoting a lesser status. However, the term "guard" is an ancient and honorable one, with roots that go back to antiquity. In addition, it is also recognized as a job classification by the federal government. In writing a book that I hope will have applications for a wide range of security forces, I have chosen the more generic term.

No book is the sole product of the author and my thanks to the many professionals who provided advice or contributions. I would particularly like to thank the staff at the O.P. Norton Resources Center of the American Society for Industrial Security, especially Eva Giercuszkiewicz and Tracy Lopez. I was not only accorded highly professional advice and assistance, but always received a warm welcome as well. Edward Guy, John Merrigan, and John Wanat kindly granted permission to reproduce the forms used in chapters 6, 8, and 10. Kevin Schild, owner of the Commercial Detective Agency of North Arlington, N.J., a friend and professional colleague for many years, came through with photos, ideas, and enthusiasm when all other sources had failed me, as he always does. And a special thank you to the staff at Butterworth-Heinemann, particularly Laurel DeWolf and Liz McCarthy, for their incredible patience with my often unpredictable schedule.

1

Organization and Function

Guard Force Functions

Like Topsy in *Uncle Tom's Cabin*, many security companies just "growed." They began as small operations, which expanded into organizational nightmares. Sooner or later, the survival of the company required a reorganization that was painful and disruptive. Sadly, much of this disruption could have been avoided if the organization had, at its inception, focused on the necessary tasks and functions that need to be performed throughout the life of a company.

Peter Drucker, in his landmark book, *Management: Tasks, Responsibilities, Practices*, points out that "organization does not start with structure but with building blocks; . . . each enterprise needs to design around the key activities appropriate to its mission and its strategies" (Drucker, 1974, p. 517). By focusing on function rather than organization, the guard company can position itself to adapt to future growth. Despite differences in size and organization, there is a commonality of function among all guard companies. The degree to which the common functions are carried out depends on whether the company is large or small, a sole proprietorship or part of a large national company. How well these functions are executed determines how well the guard company performs.

The basic functions in any guard company are as follows:

1

Management. The success or failure of a company is frequently traced to quality of management. Management has the task of unifying all the organization's functions by providing planning, organization, direction, and control. It is management that sets the goals and establishes the standards for the organization.

Administration. In any security function, there are routine administrative matters that must handled. Reports must be typed and filed, letters replied to, telephones answered. Insurance coverage must be obtained. The company must comply with laws and regulations. Although the administrative function is frequently taken for granted, its effectiveness can make or break a company.

Sales and Marketing. To survive, a company needs a continuing influx of new business. The sales and marketing function provides this through a process of promotion and positioning, client contacts, and contract negotiations.

Accounting. A guard company is a business like any other in that it makes and spends money. Because profit margins are thin in the security services business, costs must be carefully projected, clients properly billed, and guards correctly paid. The watchdog of profitability in the guard company is the accounting function.

Personnel. Guard force management by its very nature is people-oriented. The personnel function recruits the men and women that form the guard force and administers the company requirements for selection, licensing, and initial training. The personnel function is also responsible for disciplinary action, terminations, and retention.

Operations. The operations function translates policies and standards into procedures. It takes the requirements of the client and develops a staffing plan. It staffs the guard posts according to this plan and oversees the fulfillment of the guard contract. This involves the development of plans, scheduling, and dispatching, the writing of post orders, and the reviewing of guard reports.

Logistics. Guards are generally uniformed and require the use of special equipment such as flashlights and radios. The logistics function procures this equipment and issues it according to company policies and procedures. Accountability for this property is critical to the cost-effective management of any guard force.

Training. This function is sometimes placed under operations and sometimes under personnel. In truth, it is everyone's responsibility. It must address preassignment or orientation training, site-specific or on-the-job training, and continuing education.

Supervision. This function is a shared responsibility that must be taken seriously by all levels of the company. Generally, day-to-day field

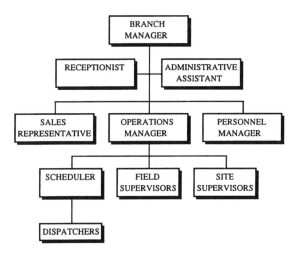

Figure 1.1 Small guard company.

supervision takes place under operations. However, all levels of management must be involved to some degree in quality control through supervision.

Figure 1.1 represents a typical small contract guard company organization. Note that functions are combined, with one person handling several different jobs. The personnel manager, for example, would not only interview candidates but would also perform background investigations, conduct preassignment training, and issue uniforms and equipment. In a larger organization, such as that depicted in Figure 1.2, these functions would be performed by several different people.

Figure 1.3 shows the structure of a typical proprietary guard force and its relationship to the rest of the organization. In this case, a director of security reports to the vice-president for operations, but the security director could just as easily be a vice-president for security reporting directly to the president. What is worth noting, however, is that many of the functions performed directly by the contract guard force are spread throughout other departments in the proprietary organization. For example, the personnel department would do the recruiting, in-processing, and initial training of the guard. Background screening would be done by the investigations department. Payroll would be handled by finance. Supervision and on-the-job training would be handled by the security department. While most proprietary guard forces do not have a sales and marketing department, several firms have been highly successful in contracting out the services of their proprietary force both within the organization and to clients outside the parent firm.

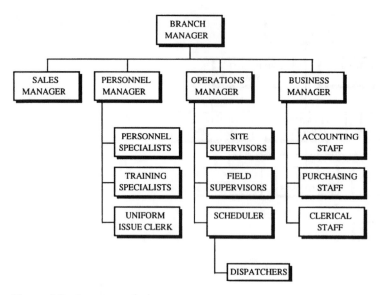

Figure 1.2   Large guard company.

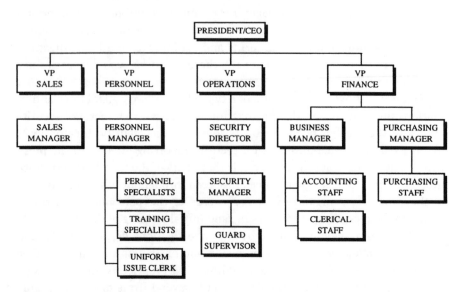

Figure 1.3   Proprietary guard force.

Note that in all three of the cases shown in Figures 1.1 through 1.3, the basic functions remain the same. The successful guard force manager must understand each of these elements and how they interrelate. While operations tends to draw much of a manager's time, it is critical that attention be given to those functions that directly support operations, such as personnel and logistics. In addition, managers who ignore accounting functions have no yardstick against which to measure success or failure and will usually experience the latter in rapid order. All the functions listed above are important—they are the heart and soul of a successful guard operation.

Guard Force Organization

To successfully market contract services, the guard company manager must understand how guard forces are organized, what force composition options (contract, proprietary, or mixed) are available, and what strengths and weaknesses exist within each type of organization. Guard forces generally fall into two categories:

Proprietary. Guards are employees of the organization to which they are providing protective services.
Contract. Guards are employees of a separate organization, which has accepted a contract to provide protective services to a particular client.

The pros and cons of each type of guard force are the source of endless discussion among security professionals. Proponents of proprietary forces cite the control that the employer has over quality of personnel, better benefits, promotion opportunities, better retention, and so forth. Contract operators counter with arguments about flexibility and economy. Both types of guard forces possess advantages and disadvantages.

Proprietary Guard Forces

A proprietary force is part of the protected organization's work force. As such, the organization can control hiring standards and insist on conformity with existing company hiring policies and practices. Salaries are usually on a par with other positions within the organization and benefits packages are identical with those of other employees. There are also possibilities for undergoing company training and for advancement into other positions within the company, including those outside the security department. Security staff members become extremely knowledgeable about the company and its operations. All of these factors tend to improve the retention rate of proprietary guards as opposed to contract guards.

The proprietary guard force does have some drawbacks. Familiarity with the company can create the potential for inadequate enforcement of rules and regulations and open up the possibility for collusion in employee theft. In addition, the proprietary force may lack the flexibility for rapid expansion and contraction to meet unusual, temporary needs, such as a labor strike. Since the size of the proprietary force must be justified on company budgets, it will generally be sized to meet only normal requirements and may be taxed to cover special events, sick days, or vacations. Recruitment and training costs must be borne by the organization. Finally, the cost of guard salaries plus benefits may not be as cost-effective as the hiring of a contract guard.

Contract Guard Forces

Contract firms offer flexibility at an affordable price. As part of the contract, the organization requiring services is provided with a guard who has received a certain number of hours of basic training plus additional site-specific training. A level of supervision by the contractor's management staff is usually part of the contract. A client can also require that potential guards be interviewed by the client's own staff prior to assignment to a facility.

Because of the size of its staff, a contracting firm can provide trained replacements for sick or unavailable officers. It can also, with adequate notice, provide an expanded staff for special events. The guard company's management team usually possesses sufficient expertise to serve as advisors or consultants on force management issues and may possess valuable contacts among public law enforcement agencies. There is also a shift in liability when a contract force is used, with a great deal of the risk being assumed by the contractor.

Like the proprietary force, the contract force can generate its own set of problems. If the contracting organization is not watchful, the quality of guard provided may not be acceptable. Some security contractors make it a practice to staff a new account with quality guards who are quickly replaced by new hires or lesser-quality guards once the initial start-up has been accomplished. Entry-level training and site-specific training for guards may be minimal or nonexistent. Many guard company "managers" are entry-level trainees with little or no security experience or training.

Deciding Between Contract and Proprietary Forces

The choice between proprietary or contract guard services appears to be one of quality control versus flexibility and cost. The decision is not so clear-cut, however. Both proprietary forces and contractor firms with good management can meet the needs of a company.

Several factors influence a client's decision between proprietary and contract guard forces.

Number of Guards

Generally speaking, large guard forces (approximately twenty or more) favor the use of contract companies (Healy & Walsh, 1983, p. 151–152). Clients requiring large forces realize a cost savings through the use of contract guards because the cost per hour of contract guards is generally lower than that for proprietary guards. It is possible to substantially reduce costs by replacing all or some of the proprietary guards with contract personnel. Conversely, a small proprietary force may not have sufficient depth and flexibility to cover sick days, vacations, and special events without some degradation of service. Such a situation would also favor the use of contract guards.

Nature of Duties

Simple duties can be performed by a contract guard with only a few hours of site training. Complex duties that require extensive training and post experience are best performed by employees who can be expected to remain with the organization for a long period of time. While a contract guard company can provide this type of guard through careful contract negotiation and planning, a site with complex responsibilities tends to favor the use of proprietary guards.

Quality of Available Supervision

Guards, whether contract or proprietary, must be supervised. If management has elected a proprietary force, this supervision requirement can be extensive, including both management and first-line supervision. A contract guard force may significantly reduce (but not totally eliminate!) these supervisory requirements.

Local Job Market

Both proprietary and contract guard forces draw from the same local labor pool. In an area with low unemployment, proprietary firms with existing benefits packages and higher salaries have a significant advantage in attracting quality candidates. Higher wages and benefits packages—necessary for a contract guard company to attract the best candidates—may increase the contract company's costs to the point where it is no longer competitive with a proprietary force. If the labor pool is large, a contract force may be more cost-effective, since salaries will be lower and benefits packages may not be necessary.

Budget Requirements

All security operations operate on constrained budgets. Consequently, the cost of the contract force versus a proprietary one is another factor that must be taken into consideration. The average contract guard who earns a lower wage and does not receive any benefits will be cheaper than the proprietary guard. However, as contracts become more elaborate, with pay steps, bonuses, benefits, and training, the cost of the contract guard approaches that of the proprietary guard.

The Combined Proprietary/Contract Force

Not all security positions require the same abilities. Some guards will perform only simple tasks, such as checking identification at entry points. Other guards will perform more complex tasks such as responding to alarms or monitoring security consoles. By combining the strengths of both the contract and proprietary force, it is possible to achieve a cost-effective mix that minimizes the weaknesses of both.

In its most basic form, the combined force uses contract employees for simpler tasks and proprietary employees for more complex ones. Organizations that have few proprietary guards may choose to augment their staff with contract guards. For example, the University of the Pacific School of Dentistry in San Francisco supplements its small staff of highly trained proprietary officers by using contract guards during vacations and special events. The contract employees form a flexible manpower reserve that can be used to relieve the proprietary officers from routine assignments to allow them to be used for special activities. The contract guards are also used when additional personnel are required for special events and work under the supervision of the proprietary officers.

Other organizations use proprietary supervisors and a contract labor pool. The Zale Corporation distribution center in New York used such a system to allow for a frequent rotation of guard staff to avoid any possibility of collusion in employee theft. A carefully selected and screened employee supervised a team of contract guards who checked out-going property and manned the metal detectors at the employee exit. Every few months, these contract guards were rotated, and new ones were brought in to reduce the chance of collusion and to keep the guards fresh and alert while performing a routine task.

The Community College of Pennsylvania also uses a combined force. In this case, the director of security and most of the guard force are employees of a contract security company. The director has responsibility for both the contract and proprietary guards used on campus.

A "layered" approach is becoming common in many organizations. Contract officers are used for routine tasks, such as the monitoring of access control points. Uniformed proprietary personnel respond to unusual occurrences and perform tasks requiring a greater degree of training than that given to the contract guards. A third level of security guard consists of senior employees who supervise the uniformed guards and perform tasks such as surveillance or initial investigations.

The Future of Contract Guard Services

The outlook for the guard business is a bright one. While the number of guards at individual sites has tended to decrease as new security technology is developed, the overall number of guards employed in the United States has continued to steadily increase. The age of the average guard is considerably lower than that of guards twenty years ago, and the average level of education is higher. The percentage of women in guard positions has increased (Cunningham & Taylor, 1984). While the number of contract guards versus proprietary guards was approximately even in 1990 (520,000 to 528,000), the number of contract guards is expected to rise to 750,000 by the year 2000, while the number of proprietary guards is projected to decrease to 410,000 (Chernicoff, March 1991, p. 46).

The guard's job has changed as well. There is more demand for guards with the ability to comprehend and use the new security technology. It is not uncommon to find guards working with access control computer systems and complex closed circuit television (CCTV) arrays. As the size of individual guard forces decrease, clients will tend to demand better-quality guards. This presents opportunities for the company specializing in premium guard service.

An additional trend has been the gradual replacement of proprietary forces by contract forces (Chernicoff, September 1991, p. 48). With increasing pressure to reduce operating budgets, security professionals must carefully weigh all available options for guard forces. Frequently, the cost savings from replacing all or part of a proprietary force with contract guards offer a significant budgetary advantage.

Another area of opportunity for contract companies is the increasing privatization of public security agencies and the replacement of public safety personnel with security guards in routine or low threat roles. Again, the emphasis is on reducing operating costs. Privatization already exists in terms of support services for public agencies, such as towing, training, and technical services. Using contract employees to free trained public employees for more important duties is a logical step in times of strained public budgets. Contract security personnel are being used for traffic and parking control, prisoner escort, securing crime scenes, and court protection duties. In a precedent-setting move, the state of Florida contracted with Wackenhut to supply security for fifty-nine rest stops throughout the state, a task previously performed by three separate state agencies (Elig, 1993, p.1).

In certain areas, the private sector is sometimes willing to fund the use of contract personnel for jobs traditionally done by public employees. In New York City, a group of businessmen became concerned about the effect of criminal attacks on the tourist trade. These businessmen formed a nonprofit organization that receives a special tax collected by the city. The organization then hired forty-two guards to patrol the Times Square area of New York City. Since the program was implemented, overall crime in the area has decreased by twenty-three percent (Marquis, 1994, p. 10).

One area of concern is the increase in legislation aimed at creating standards and minimum requirements for the guard industry. While many guard company owners resist such legislation because of the potential for increased costs, clearly national standards of some sort are greatly needed in the industry. The question is whether the industry will become self-policing or whether government will dictate such requirements with laws framed by legislators with no knowledge of the industry. A third alternative is a partnership between the industry's professional associations such as the American Society for Industrial Security and legislators willing to author bills needed by guard companies to better police themselves.

Nevertheless, contract guard companies that position themselves to take advantage of emerging growth opportunities will profit in the future. The starting point for this growth is the development of intelligent and flexible management practices.

2

Management

Frequently, a guard company hired to replace a substandard contractor recruits the majority of the outgoing firm's employees and provides satisfactory service. A proprietary force that is performing poorly is revitalized by a new manager and begins producing quality work. Two guard companies draw employees from the same labor pool; one company has a reputation for providing excellent guards, the other for providing poor service. How is this possible? The answer lies in the application of sound management principles.

The problem with many guard companies is not that the guards are poor performers. After all, companies recruit from essentially the same labor pool. Instead, guard companies that perform poorly are, in fact, frequently poorly managed.

There are four primary functions of management: control, planning, organizing, and directing. Together they form a management cycle in which each function builds on the other.

Control is accomplished by establishing the goals, policies, and standards that guide the organization and focus its activities. Each employee of the company must know where the company is going and what corporate values are acceptable. This understanding of common goals fosters a cohesiveness within the organization that is critical for success.

Planning is the development of the strategy to achieve the company's goals. This involves the establishment of specific objectives derived from those goals. Planning requires clarity of vision and the ability to focus on where the company will be in the future, not where it is today. U.S. corporations have traditionally focused on short-term goals, such as annual sales. Japanese firms, by contrast, focus on five-, ten-, and even twenty-year periods, aiming for market position rather than short-term advantages.

Organization identifies the people and resources needed to achieve planned goals and objectives. It clarifies lines of authority and apportions responsibility. The organizational structure of a company determines the operating environment for that organization. Studies have shown that employees function well in environments that foster personal growth and responsibility. They do poorly in organizations that micromanage.

Direction includes the assignment and coordination of specific objectives and the oversight necessary to ensure that objectives are met. Management must provide clear and final decisions on critical issues. Day-to-day decisions should be deferred to the appropriate staff level. However, when a decision is such that it can only be made by management, that decision should be made swiftly and decisively.

Control

Goals and the Vision Statement

A major problem in many companies is that management has never clearly defined where it wants to take the organization. Instead, the focus is on short-term milestones and day-to-day operations. A company becomes more concerned about quarterly projections than about a two- or five-year plan. The focus is on staffing a single post for the night rather than increasing market share.

It is critical that the guard company manager articulate clear and easily understood goals for the company. The first goal that springs to mind is, of course, quality of service. It is too easy, however, to say "we will provide the best service possible to our clients." What about other variables? For example, what part does cost-effectiveness or profit play in the organization? Is profit or service the reason for the organization? Is there a balance? Perhaps a more realistic goal is to "maximize profit while providing service to our clients that meets acceptable standards."

The goals of the organization are usually summarized in what is known as the "mission statement." It has become popular lately in large corporations to refer to the mission statement as the organization's "vision statement," and this is perhaps more descriptive of what needs to be accomplished in setting goals for the organization. Developing a vision statement is not an easy task and requires a great deal of thought on the part of management. The vision statement should be realistic, honest, and attainable.

Code of Ethics

Another way management can convey its intentions is through the use of an organizational code of ethics. *Private Security: Report of the Task Force on Private Security* (National Advisory Committee on Criminal Justice Standards and Goals, 1976) defined a code of ethics as "a statement that incorporates moral and ethical principles and philosophies." Many organizations choose to incorporate these principles in the vision statement; others use a separate document. The code of ethics is designed to provide guidance to the employee in dealing with situations not specifically covered in written instructions. It provides a standard against which an employee's behavior and actions can be measured.

While it is possible for the organization to develop its own code of ethics, many companies adopt industry standards. For example, many security managers adopt the Code of Ethics of the American Society for Industrial Security (ASIS); just as many security consultants voluntarily adopt the Code of the International Association of Professional Security Consultants (IAPSC). The Task Force on Private Security, cited earlier, developed two codes of ethics: one for security managers and one for security employees. While the security manager's code has been largely superseded by the more succinct code adopted by ASIS, the security employee's code of ethics remains one of the best written specifically for security guards. (See Figure 2.1.)

As with the vision statement, the policies and procedures of the organization must reflect the code of ethics. To develop a policy that conflicts with the code invalidates the whole code in the eyes of the employees. Once adopted, a code of ethics must serve as a guide for every activity within the organization. Consequently, any proposed code should be carefully examined and discussed before being implemented.

Policies and Procedures

In order to attain his or her objectives, an effective manager must explain *how* work is to be accomplished. This is the function of organizational policies. A policy embodies management's guidelines for dealing with a specific issue. It can be used to establish a program or to reflect concerns over a particular issue. An example of the former is a policy directive that establishes an organizational safety program. An example of the latter is a policy on equal opportunity hiring practices.

Policies are particularly important to the guard force organization. Besides accomplishing their primary purpose—to communicate to subordinates the intentions of management—policy documents also play an important role in liability litigation and can be used to demonstrate management's con-

---

Code of Ethics for Private Security Employees

In recognition of the significant contribution of private security to crime prevention and reduction, as a private security employee, I pledge:

I.   To accept the responsibilities and fulfill the obligations of my role: protecting life and property; preventing and reducing crimes against my employer's business, or other organizations and institutions to which I am assigned; upholding the law; and respecting the constitutional rights of all persons.

II.   To conduct myself with honesty and integrity and to adhere to the highest moral principles in the performance of my security duties.

III.   To be faithful, diligent, and dependable in discharging my duties and to uphold at all times the laws, policies, and procedures that protect the rights of others.

IV.   To observe the precepts of truth, accuracy, and prudence, without allowing personal feelings, prejudices, animosities, or friendships to influence my judgment.

V.   To report to my superiors, without hesitation, any violation of the law or of my employer's or client's regulations.

VI.   To respect and protect the confidential and privileged information of my employer or client beyond the term of my employment, except where their interests are contrary to law or to this Code of Ethics.

VII.   To cooperate with all recognized and responsible law enforcement and government agencies in matters within their jurisdiction.

VIII.   To accept no compensation, commission, gratuity, or other advantage without the knowledge and consent of my employer.

IX.   To conduct myself professionally at all times and to perform my duties in a manner that reflects credit upon myself, my employer, and private security.

X.   To strive continually to improve my performance by seeking training and educational opportunities that will better prepare me for my private security duties.

Figure 2.1   The Task Force on Private Security Code of Ethics.

cern or disregard for a particular issue. For example, if a guard organization is being sued for false arrest, the organization that has a published arrest policy is in a better position to defend itself than the organization that has no policy. In the absence of written guidelines, it is difficult to prove that a guard was acting outside established organizational policy.

Policy documents should not be confused with operational memoranda. Too frequently, an organization issues a new "policy" by sending a memorandum to all employees. However, this memorandum is not filed as a reference for future employees, and anyone researching organizational policy will be lucky to locate it. Policies should be numbered for reference, should follow the same format, and should be incorporated into an organizational policy manual.

Policy documents should include six basic items:

1. *A reference number* to allow the document to be readily located. Large corporations use an alphanumeric system to group policies by function, e.g., all policies referring to personnel would be found under the letter B. A policy giving guidance on the hiring of minorities might be designated B-12.

2. *A title* describing the policy's main focus. Since the title will determine where the policy is filed and whether or not it can be easily found, careful consideration should be given to selecting a title. For example, "Firearms Policy for Security Personnel " tells the reader much more than "Security Policy Directive #3."

3. *A statement of concern*, answering the question of why the organization considers the policy important. This is a brief statement explaining the reasons behind the policy and the desired result of its implementation. It is also appropriate to highlight any connections to the company's code of ethics or vision statement.

4. *General guidance* regarding the policy issue. Note that the policy is not specific in the sense of telling the reader exactly how to accomplish a task but provides general guidelines. An accident policy would state that an accident report must be submitted after any accident. It will not tell the reader what form to use or how to submit the report.

5. *An authorizing signature* to avoid the proliferation of "policies." It is important to delegate the issuance of policy directives only to key management personnel.

6. *A date of implementation.* To keep policies current, they should be reviewed on a regular basis and updated as needed. Generally, a well-written policy will not need to be changed very frequently. Some organizations, however, ensure that policies are current by requiring that they be reviewed and reissued every two to five years.

A policy provides broad guidance and communicates the manager's intentions. Procedures explain exactly how policy is to be implemented. To use the example just cited, an organization's policy dictates that an accident report be prepared after each accident involving an employee. It does not give specifics on how this is to be accomplished. A procedural document provides information on how to implement the policy. Such a document includes the specific form to be used, what information is required, and how many copies are prepared and to whom they are submitted.

Policy is the province of upper management. Procedures, however, are best developed by staff who will be required to implement the policy. For example, if a policy states that security guards may not work over twelve hours in a twenty-four-hour period, the operations manager should develop the specific instructions that tell the dispatcher and scheduler how to effect a relief, how to find replacements, what constitutes an adequate rest period, and so forth.

Because situations change, procedures need to be kept current. Consequently, the life cycle of a procedure is generally much shorter than that of a policy. Taking the example of the accident report, if the organization reorganizes and changes the reporting channels, the procedure needs to be revised. Note that the *policy* to submit the report has not changed, only the implementing *procedures*. Likewise, the issuance of a new form or a change in state reporting requirements would also require a revision to the procedures. As these examples demonstrate, procedures need to be reviewed frequently, with an annual review recommended.

Procedures are usually filed with the policy that generated them in the policy and procedures manual. Thus, an employee with a specific question can use the index to find the appropriate policy and its implementing procedures in one location.

Policies are written as general guidelines with procedures outlining implementation. They are by nature difficult to adjust on a daily basis. Many organizations use memoranda to deal with interim changes or one-time events that require an adjustment. It is essential, however, that memoranda not be used to replace the revision of an outdated policy or procedure.

Standards and Codes

It would be difficult and unnecessary to issue each employee a full copy of the policy and procedures manual. Many of the items in the manual refer to specific issues that are not addressed on a daily basis by the rank-and-file employee. Further, keeping track of the manuals and issuing changes would rapidly become an administrative nightmare. How then does management communicate its intent as to what constitutes acceptable organizational behavior?

To address this issue, organizational standards are derived from policies and procedures. For example, the policy and procedures for an accident can be reduced to the standard "If you are injured on the job, notify your supervisor immediately." A policy requiring all guards to wear the appropriate uniform may be implemented by procedures telling the logistics staff what type of uniform to purchase and how many sets to issue to each guard. The standard tells the guard that he or she must be in uniform and what constitutes the uniform.

Standards are critical. Many employees need to see requirements in writing before they will perform specific tasks. Written standards add weight to the corrections made by a supervisor. In short, standards tell the employee what he or she must know, be, and do to meet the minimum acceptable standards in the company. The standards must be in writing and must be provided to each employee. It is also important, in terms of liability litigation, to prove that the employee received a copy of the standards. With guards, it is easy to make the written standards an item of issue like the uniform and record their issuance on the appropriate document.

Standards, like policies, should be guidelines that are relatively resistant to change. Like procedures, however, they must contain enough specificity that the employee knows what is expected. Guard organizations sometimes refer to standards as general orders and issue them in the form of a booklet that can be carried by each guard. This is particularly effective if the booklet becomes an item of inspection when the guard is checked by a supervisor and when the supervisor periodically questions the guard on its contents.

Policies Affecting Liability

In accepting a contract to provide protective services, the guard company also accepts a portion of the client's liability. The client will always be held to have a duty to provide adequate security, but the risk is now shared with the guard company. In a lawsuit, the exact apportionment of civil damages would be determined by the jury.

The third party that shares the risk is the security guard. If the guard is held to have been performing within the scope of his or her employment, the guard company must accept full responsibility for the guard's actions. It is in the best interest of the guard company, therefore, to define, prior to an incident, what constitutes "scope of employment."

While it would be difficult to list every policy that must be formulated by a guard company, there are several that are fairly standard in the security industry. The following are examples of the type of policy issues that need to be decided by management and then recorded in written policy guidance:

1. *Arrest Procedures.* Nowhere is the risk of a civil suit greater than when a security guard makes an arrest. Potential causes of action in a civil suit can range from false arrest and wrongful imprisonment to excessive use of force. Some guard companies avoid this problem by forbidding the guard to make an arrest under any circumstances. This may not always be practical, particularly if the client is a retailer seeking to reduce shoplifting. If the company does permit arrests, there should be a clear policy regarding the circumstances under which an arrest can be made. Implementing proce-

dures should describe how an arrest should be handled. The policy should also address mandatory training requirements on arrest procedures prior to assignment.

2. *Use of Force.* How far can a guard go in enforcing the client's wishes or in effecting an arrest? What about self-defense or defense of the client's employees? If no policy covers these issues, the guard company can be found negligent for failing to anticipate them. The use-of-force policy should cover the use of weapons, both lethal and nonlethal, and of restraint devices, such as handcuffs. It must also address the specific use of lethal force.

3. *Search and Seizure.* Many guards have the responsibility for checking employees entering or leaving a facility. It is important that they understand what is an appropriate method for searching and confiscating contraband, particularly if an arrest and prosecution are involved. Recently, a security guard in a California public school created an enormous amount of controversy by conducting a strip search of all the male juveniles in a particular class. The "stolen" money that the guard was searching for was later found to have been misplaced and not stolen at all.

4. *Responding to Emergencies.* Security guards must deal with unexpected emergencies on a regular basis. Whenever a guard does so, there is a liability risk. Consequently, the guard company should have a specific policy for dealing with each type of likely emergency. For example, if guards are expected to render first aid, the policy should address the circumstances under which they will do so and the required training that must be given to them. Fires are a major problem that all guards must deal with. Does the company want the guard to use a fire extinguisher on a small fire? Should the fire department be contacted for all fires? Liability exists either way. The guard company management must decide what is a reasonable policy to protect the guard, the company, and the client.

5. *Catastrophic Events.* What happens in the event of an earthquake or severe winter storm? Does the guard leave the post or remain on duty? For how long? How do dispatchers and supervisors react? Again, decisions on these issues are best made before the event.

6. *Conduct on Post.* Surprisingly, many companies do not have a policy that tells a guard what is expected of him or her on post. This policy should include prohibitions on theft, solicitation of employment, abuse of client property, and similar actions that serve to discredit the guard company. It might also address issues such as reading or studying on post.

7. *Disciplinary Actions.* As part of its commitment to fair employment practices, the company should have a formal way to deal with disciplinary problems. Such a policy would specify what infractions are grounds for immediate dismissal, who has the authority to terminate, how lesser offenses are handled, and how the guard can appeal an adverse action. If the company is unionized, this policy might explain grievance procedures as well.

   8. *Administrative Policies.* Many policies deal with routine administrative matters. For example, the company may have an overtime policy that limits the amount of hours a guard can work. Other policies include uniform and equipment issue, wearing of uniforms, reporting, sick leave, vacation, use of company vehicles, safeguarding client keys, and payroll complaints. There are other policies that may be mandated by statutes such as OSHA regulations, equal employment opportunity laws, and state labor laws.

Planning

Long-Range versus Short-Range Planning

   Traditionally, planning in American companies usually consists of an annual budget projection. On the other hand, Japanese corporations, as mentioned earlier, develop longer-term projections. This allows the Japanese company to work toward a predetermined goal as part of a long-range plan. Although plans will be altered and modified as market factors change, the overall goal will remain as a guide to all individual effort.

   It is important to note that the long-range and short-range plans must be fully integrated and mutually supporting. The long-range plan ultimately grows out of the intermediate short-range plans. Further, "short" and "long" do not necessarily refer to the actual time required to implement a plan but rather the period of its effect. A decision made by a company that affects its operations for the next several years is definitely long-term, even if it took only a few months to implement.

Strategic Plans

   Plans are generally of two types: *operational plans* that focus on short-term objectives and *strategic plans* that have long-range impact on company operations. Operational plans are characterized by specific performance objectives and time frames, usually of one year or less. One of the basic operational plans used by all companies is the annual budget (see chapter 7). Strategic plans are wider in scope, focusing on ways of achieving broad goals rather than specific objectives, and usually cover multiyear periods.

   Drucker (Drucker, 1974) points out that there are three basic questions that must be asked in strategic planning: What is our business? What will it be? What should it be? In answering these questions, the guard company brings into focus all the factors necessary for strategic planning. For instance, is our business only security guards or should we sell other services, such as physical security consulting? Should we expand or eliminate the consulting service? Should we diversify?

A frequent problem with long-range planning is the tendency to try to predict the future and develop plans based on these predictions. The tremendous market changes of the past few years, brought about by the collapse of the Eastern Block and by the Gulf War, demonstrate the fallacy of this approach. Instead, a company must develop a systematic process for making decisions that incorporates an analysis of the future impact of those decisions. This process must also accept that the current way of doing business in the company will probably not be sufficient in the future and must encourage the development of new ways to deliver service.

The National Management Association's *Handbook for Managers* recommends a five-step process for strategic planning (Virga, 1987, p. 39).

1. *Analyze your situation.* Look at your company first—its strengths and weaknesses. How is it positioned? What does it do well or poorly? What resources does it have or expect to have? Follow this with a study of external factors using analytical tools such as the market study described in chapter 4. Since strategic plans by their nature look to the future, accurate forecasting is critical. This should include both objective forecasting (studying past events and extrapolating to the future) and subjective forecasting (pooling knowledge and experience to predict likely future events) as well as economic forecasting.

2. *Define your goals.* Given your company's present and projected situation and the external factors that you have analyzed, what is it you want to accomplish? Identifying far-reaching but specific goals involves the balancing of opportunity and risk. Frequently, the decision to adopt a specific goal means that other opportunities will be missed. Once the decision is made, however, these goals must be clearly stated.

3. *Select a strategy.* By this point, the planner should have identified possible ways of achieving the desired goals. These strategies can be analyzed (see the discussion on the decision-making process that follows) and the best strategy for each goal selected. Again, competing strategies will involve trade-offs and careful risk analysis.

4. *Set policy guidelines.* This step relates to the function of controlling discussed earlier. Policies provide the decision-making framework that guides the activities of subordinates. They ensure a unity of effort that allows the goals of the company to be achieved.

5. *Develop action plans and programs.* This relates to the function of directing, which will be discussed later in this chapter. Within the policy guidelines established in step 4, managers develop objectives needed to implement the agreed-upon strategy. These objectives are specific and measurable.

The guard business is competitive and dynamic, with conditions often changing on a daily basis. It is important to develop long-range goals that will smooth out the erratic fluctuations of the marketplace. For example, failure to meet an annual projection can be placed into perspective if it is viewed in the context of a five-year plan to increase market share. Since the goal is to increase market share rather than make a short-term profit, the acquisition of several key clients over time might tend to offset the temporary loss of revenue from the failure to win numerous small contracts. The company must look at the overall picture rather than just the apparent short-term failure.

Operational Plans

The Japanese realize that the plan itself is not as important as the planning process, and this holds true for the guard company. To develop a plan requires that management set goals, as was discussed in the first part of this chapter. Once the goals are established, the organization has a clear picture of *where* it is going. Objectives derived from these goals tell an organization *what* it is going to do to get there. Where a goal is fairly broad in scope, an objective is specific and tied to a quarterly or annual time frame. The contract firm can quantify objectives fairly easily—it is simple to set objectives for the increase of guard hours sold, potential clients contacted, or personnel recruited. Objectives can also be slightly more creative—costs reduced, number of incidents resolved, conflicts avoided, personnel trained. Whatever the objectives selected, they must be realistic, attainable, specific, and clearly communicated to the guard force.

Since objectives are based on the goals of the business, they highlight the contribution of each employee to the advancement of the company, while allowing for teamwork and creativity. The result is increased productivity, which means increased profits. Drucker (1974, pp. 95–100) cites several examples of the effectiveness of objective setting, most notably the rapid growth of Marks & Spencer.

Objectives make up the basic business strategy of the company and must therefore be derived from the company's goals. While goals are visionary, objectives are operational, concentrating personnel and resources on specific desired results. Drucker (1974, p. 100) recommends that objectives be defined for eight areas that he considers essential for the survival of any company:

Marketing
Innovation
Human Organization
Financial Resources
Physical Resources
Productivity
Social Responsibility
Profit Requirements

The development of objectives should be a team effort involving both management and the individual who will have to meet the objectives. For example, if the objective is an increase of sales, the salesman who must meet the objective should provide input on what is a realistic percentage of increase. If management does not agree, a dialogue should take place until both sides agree on the objectives and the time frame involved.

Frequently, an organization will subdivide objectives into measurable milestones. These are merely indicators that demonstrate how close an organization is to meeting its objectives. For example, if an objective is to have all guards retrained in a specific task by the end of the year, it may be appropriate to set milestones for the number to be trained each quarter. However, milestones are only indicators and therefore flexible. They should not be used as an evaluation tool the way objectives are but merely to measure progress and generate discussion.

Establishing goals and establishing objectives are the first two steps in the process known as "management by objectives" (MBO). The remainder of the MBO process requires a commitment from the manager to periodically review progress of the subordinate and to allow the subordinate freedom of action in meeting those objectives. This involves a certain amount of risk taking—the manager must trust the subordinate to accomplish the task. The planning process requires that the manager and subordinate mutually agree on the objective and on an action plan developed by the subordinate. This action plan becomes part of the review and evaluation process discussed in chapter 5.

Organizing

Management Principles

The organization of any company must be based on sound management principles. Without this base, it is possible to develop an organizational structure that is inefficient at best and self-destructive at worst. The principles of organizational management are well known and can be found in any basic text on management. They are as follows:

1. *Assignment of Responsibility.* In any company, there are tasks that must be accomplished. Someone must be responsible for the accomplishment of each task. A function of management is to clearly define the tasks to be done and to assign specific individuals to accomplish them.

2. *Delegation of Authority.* In order to accomplish an assigned task, an individual must have the authority to carry out the functions necessary to complete the task. If all authority is centralized in a single individual who must be consulted before any decision is made, the company will lose its ability to react quickly to changing market demands. Consequently, management must develop clearly identified lines of authority commensurate with assigned responsibility.

3. *Span of Control.* There is a limit to the number of individuals one person can directly supervise. If too many subordinates and responsibilities are assigned to an individual, it becomes physically impossible to adequately control and coordinate activities. The maximum number of subordinates that an individual can supervise will vary with the individual and the complexity of the responsibilities he or she is assigned. Charles Sennewald, in his book *Effective Security Management* (1978), suggests that this number is no more than five for upper-level management and twelve for lower-level supervisors. This tallies with the experience of emergency services personnel under the Incident Command System, the standardized organizational structure used to respond to fires, police incidents, and disasters. It is also consistent with the span of control used by the U.S. Army. Note that this relates to *direct* supervision, not overall responsibility. For example, a supervisor might be responsible for a hundred guards but only directly supervise four shift leaders.

4. *Unity of Command.* This is a basic principle that is often overlooked. Simply stated, it means that an individual should work for only one supervisor. The employee must perceive a clear line of authority that flows from senior management through the supervisor. Upholding this principle requires a commitment from management to work through the chain of command and avoid going directly to an employee. Similarly, the employee should deal with management through his or her supervisor, not directly, except in exceptional cases.

5. *Coordination of Function.* For a company to be effective, each function within the organization must complement and support the others. For example, deficiencies noted during supervisor inspections should be referred to those who can solve the problem: to personnel for disciplinary action, to training for remedial or proactive instruction, or to logistics for replacement of equipment. If each of these four functions operated independently, the deficiency might never be corrected, or the guard might begin to feel harassed when he or she was approached by several different people about the same problem.

It is the responsibility of management to ensure that functions are working together and to coordinate and direct their efforts towards the achievement of the company's goals.

Organizational Structure

There are three basic organizational structures: line, functional, and line and staff. The *line organization,* also known as the *scalar* or *military organization,* charts direct authority from the top manager to the lowest supervisor (Figure 2.2). It provides a very clear statement of lines of authority and responsibility.

In his 1947 book, *Scientific Management,* Frederick W. Taylor moved away from an organizational model using direct lines of authority and suggested that a company could be organized along functional lines. For example, all tasks related to personnel are placed under the personnel department. Under a functional organization, supervisors become specialists in a particular task and focus only on that task. The majority of companies today are organized along functional lines (Figure 2.3).

As an organization increases in size, there is often a need for specialists who can serve as advisors or provide support to line supervisors without having direct authority over those supervisors. These specialized staff functions might include training and general counsel (Figure 2.4). In addition to serving

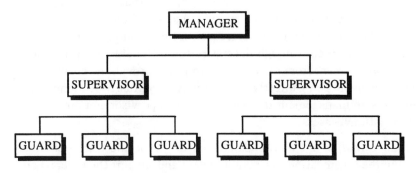

Figure 2.2 Line organization.

Figure 2.3   Functional organization.

as advisors or providing support, staff members might also serve as regulators. For example, the finance and accounting staff might develop fiscal procedures to be implemented by all other departments.

Note that all three organizational structures build on each other. The simplicity of the line organization is still very much a part of both the functional and the line and staff structures. The key to a good organizational structure is to realize how these structures blend together and to strive for simplicity.

One very basic rule is to use the minimum number of management levels possible, thereby ensuring the shortest possible chain of command. Another basic rule is to remember that, while a company may have a formal organization, an informal organization will also exist. This informal organization might arise because of the particular strengths and weaknesses of certain individuals or as the result of a change of conditions. The closer the formal and informal organizational structures are, the better the company will run. The company should not opt to reorganize to achieve this goal, however, unless conditions clearly dictate that reorganization is needed. The disruption

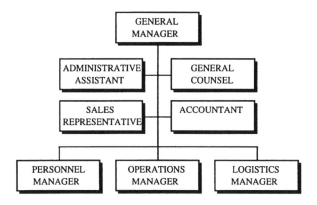

Figure 2.4   Line and staff organization.

caused by reorganization may have negative effects that are far more significant than the perceived need for change.

It is also important to remember that, as Dale and Urwick point out in *Staff in Organization* (1960), while many of the organizational principles adopted by business are based on the experience of the military, companies generally lack the cohesiveness and singleness of purpose found in the military. Consequently, it is important to keep the human factor in mind when developing an organizational structure. The emphasis must be on what works and is effective rather than on what fits the traditional framework. An example of this would be the use of a task force or committee formed for a specific purpose and dissolved as soon as the purpose is accomplished. Group decisions are often more easily accepted in an organization than those made by a single manager.

Organizational Charts

Many companies fail to formalize their organization in the form of an organizational chart. Others develop charts that are improperly laid out and confusing. The proper use of an organizational chart can go a long way to clarifying lines of authority and responsibility. It should be one of the

---

BASIC RULES FOR ORGANIZATION CHARTS

1. Keep the chart as simple as possible. Don't try to show too much and limit the use of auxiliary lines. If necessary, break the chart into a series of smaller charts.

2. Use rectangular boxes for units or personnel. Each box should show a title that is both descriptive and functional.

3. Vertical placement denotes relative position within the company and positions of equal status or rank should be treated the same. Boxes on the same horizontal row should be the same size and show only those positions of equal rank or status. Boxes at the top of the chart must always be at least as big as others lower down.

4. Lines of authority are shown by solid vertical and horizontal lines. Lines of authority always enter a box at the top and leave at the bottom except for staff positions.

5. The flow of functional authority is shown by dotted or broken lines.

Figure 2.5   Rules for organizational charts.

first things provided to a new employee and should be reissued any time there is a major change. Some companies reissue the organizational chart annually.

Charting an organization is not particularly complex, and there are several excellent computer programs that make it even simpler. There are, however, a few formal rules that must be followed. These are summarized in Figure 2.5.

Directing

Directing is done by managers on a daily basis. It involves the establishment of objectives, the motivation of employees, decision making, coordination, and innovation. It requires coordination, conflict resolution, and performance evaluation. Most of all, it requires leadership.

Leadership

There is a tremendous body of literature on the leadership role of management. Many researchers have attempted to quantify that intangible "something" that is the essence of leadership. A full discussion of leadership theory is beyond the scope of this book. However, there are some practical characteristics that should be present in a company leader.

Leadership is what Bruce Caine calls "the effective exercise of influence" (Caine, 1976). An effective leader is one who can use his or her influence to create institutional purpose while at the same time satisfying the needs and goals of subordinates. This harkens back to the earlier discussion on goals and objectives and to the principle of unity of command. The manager as leader must persuade subordinates that their needs can best be met by achieving company goals.

This type of leadership, termed "transforming leadership" by James MacGregor Burns (Peters and Waterman, 1982), carries with it a responsibility not only to the company but to the employees as well. Employees have a right to expect certain things from management, among them consistency, fairness, and decisiveness.

Consistency means dealing with similar situations in similar ways. Employees are comfortable with a management whose actions are firmly based on principles that have been defined and codified. It is relatively simple for each employee to understand what is expected of him or her and how management will react to violations of accepted standards. Consistency also promotes fairness—rules are understood and applied consistently. By being consistent and fair, managers build trust among employees.

Fairness not only pertains to dealing with actual employee problems; it involves employee perceptions as well. Employees are quick to determine when a company has a double standard that allows certain individuals more latitude than that accorded to the rank and file. While no one denies that there are perks that go along with promotion and status in a company, there is a big difference between these and blatant abuse of position. In a guard company, any perception that management is dishonest, condones abuse of client property or services, or otherwise regularly violates accepted standards will be instantly fatal for the company.

One management trait that is frequently overlooked by companies is that of decisiveness. With the delegation of authority, management has quite rightly delegated day-to-day decision making to subordinate managers and supervisors. These subordinates occasionally need to refer decisions that exceed their level of authority to management. These decisions must be acted upon quickly. Nothing can affect morale in a company as rapidly as the perception that senior-level management is incapable of making a decision.

Surprisingly, many managers have never been taught the basic decision-making model. This model is so simple as to almost be a cliché. Yet, its very simplicity is what makes it so effective a management tool. The decision-making model has five components:

1. *Recognize and define the problem.* Although it seems a logical place to start, many problem solvers waste tremendous amounts of effort by failing to clearly define a problem. Many times the issue at hand is merely the symptom of a greater problem. Other times, the real problem may not be readily apparent. The first critical step in decision making is to define the problem. It is helpful to write out this definition and refer back to it throughout the process.

2. *Gather facts and make assumptions to determine the scope of the problem and solution.* Conan Doyle's Sherlock Holmes frequently remarks to his associate, Dr. Watson, that it is useless to speculate about a problem until one is in possession of the facts. The same holds true for any type of decision making. As part of researching a problem, it may become necessary to limit or expand the scope of the original problem and solution. It will almost always be necessary to make some assumptions about the problem, particularly if it involves a financial decision.

3. *Develop possible solutions to the problem.* Creativity is the hallmark of true leadership. To solve a complex problem, it is sometimes necessary to think in new ways. In searching for a fastener for astronaut garments, NASA engineers used an unusual brainstorming technique that required them to visualize a rain forest. An engineer's image of being caught on thorns led to the development of velcro. While not all problems will require this type of problem solving, at this stage of the decision-making process all possible solutions should be considered.

4. *Analyze and compare possible solutions.* During this phase of the process, the solutions developed in the previous phase are analyzed and ranked. If it is a complex problem, competing solutions may be discussed in a group or analyzed with computer models. The goal of this phase is to eliminate unworkable or unacceptable solutions.

5. *Select the best possible solution to the problem.* In the final phase of problem solving, the best possible solution is selected from the acceptable solutions identified in the previous phase. This solution should be checked against the problem statement to be sure it really does solve the problem and then implemented.

Evaluating Progress

The company can be likened to a ship—it requires constant attention and many small adjustments to keep on course. Planning has charted the course, organization has provided a crew, and controlling has provided the rigging, but it is directing that will determine whether or not the voyage is successful. An important part of directing is the evaluation of how well the company is progressing toward the achievement of its goals. This evaluation must be based on the measurable objectives that were established during the planning process.

Managers can monitor the achievement of objectives before, during, and after the process of accomplishment. This allows the employee to receive continuous feedback and assistance. The initial phase of any project requires the employee to assemble the appropriate resources for the job. By monitoring this first phase, the manager can ensure that needed resources are present to accomplish the objective. Through continued monitoring during the process, the manager can help keep the activity on track and make corrections and suggestions as needed. Care must be taken, however, to avoid "micromanaging" or completely taking over the project. Objective accomplishment can also be determined by monitoring process output through management reports or milestones met.

The achievement of objectives must be measured against the company goals. As pointed out earlier, failure to meet an objective may not in itself represent a failure of performance. As part of the monitoring process, the manager must determine if external factors have changed in a way that requires a rethinking of objectives. It is important to determine *why* an objective was not met, and to adjust the long-range company goals if necessary.

3

Administration and Office Management

Guard company managers tend to focus most of their attention on field operations. This is understandable, as field operations generate profit, while administration is a nonbillable expense. Consequently, there is an emphasis on cost savings and keeping administrative expense to the bare minimum. Office staffs tend to be "lean and mean," with most administrative employees performing multiple jobs. However, there are a number of key administrative tasks that must be accomplished if a guard company is to survive. These tasks, while not appearing as urgent as day-to-day field operations, must nevertheless receive as much of the manager's attention as operations.

Administrative Staff

Developing the Staff

Because the administrative staff is pure overhead (i.e., a cost not billed directly to a client), guard companies tend to keep administrative staff to a minimum. This is usually accomplished by requiring entry-level managers and supervisors to perform routine clerical functions such as reception, uniform issue, and filing. While all members of a guard company must be prepared to perform multiple functions, this type of approach can be a false economy. This is particularly obvious when one compares the cost per hour of a junior manager to that of a clerical worker (Figure 3.1).

There is an additional cost. The heavy administrative burden carried by most guard companies' management staff generates a high degree of stress. As managers approach their individual burnout thresholds, this stress will manifest itself in poor employee and client relationships that can have an impact on the retention of both quality guards and clients. While the nature of the guard business generates considerable stress at the best of times, the good manager must see that this stress is kept to a reasonable level.

In developing an administrative staff, inexperienced managers tend to think in terms of full-time employees. A common reply to overburdened staff is "we can't afford to hire another worker." A good manager focuses instead on the work that needs to be done. If there is not enough work or money for a full-time employee, part-time or temporary employees can be hired. This can be particularly useful for cyclical activities such as payroll or tax periods.

Another source of part-time help is guards who are used as relief guards at several different posts. For example, the guard can work two to three days at client sites then the rest of his or her time at the office. This is a good way of observing the work habits and motivation of potential supervisors.

One creative source of staffing is developing an intern program with a community college or vocational school. Students work part-time after school or on weekends at a nominal rate of pay and are graded on the quality of their performance. Those who perform well are potential candidates for full-time positions.

If the need for additional administrative staff develops unexpectedly or if there is a need to cover for the absence of a staff member because of illness or vacation, the company can contract for a temporary worker with a number of reputable firms. While this is an added expense, it is preferable to overburden-

	HOURLY RATE	ANNUAL RATE
FILE CLERK	$6.41	$13,332.80
JUNIOR MANAGER	$10.57	$22,000.00
POTENTIAL SAVINGS	$4.16	$8,667.20

Figure 3.1   Salary comparison, manager versus clerical worker.

ing the remaining staff or letting work pile up. In addition, a good temporary employee is a potential candidate for a regular position with the guard company.

Key Staff Positions

There are several key positions that are normally found in the office staff of security companies: office manager, secretary, receptionist, and clerical worker. In smaller offices, the specific tasks performed in these positions are frequently combined, particularly the duties of secretary/receptionist/clerical worker. It is important to focus on the tasks to be performed rather than position titles and to develop appropriate position descriptions for actual office staff.

There are other personnel who are critical to the functioning of an office, such as an accountant or general counsel. These are, however, specialized services that are frequently contracted out by the average guard company and will not be covered here.

Office Manager

The office manager serves as the supervisor for all administrative staff. This may include supervising related functions such as accounting, personnel, and logistics or may be limited to clerical staff only. In addition to supervising and motivating employees, the office manager is responsible for developing and maintaining systems to accomplish the administrative tasks discussed later in this chapter. The ideal office manager not only must be a strong supervisor, but must also have an extensive knowledge of administrative systems and practices, business law, and accounting and personnel practices.

Few guard companies begin business with an office manager in place. Yet at no time is this position more critical than in the start-up phase of the company. The supervision of the staff can be accomplished as a collateral duty of another manager, as it usually is in a guard company, but it is absolutely essential that administrative management systems be developed and put in place from the first day of operations.

The guard company has several options to accomplish this, short of hiring a full-time office manager. One way is to hire a consultant for the start-up phase and for periodic review of administrative management systems. Another is the use of a part-time office manager. The most common practice, however, is to combine several administrative jobs. For example, the office manager also may serve as the personnel manager or business (accounting) manager. In small offices, he or she may also serve as secretary. Remember, however, that it is important that there be someone in the office specifically charged with developing and maintaining administrative management systems.

Secretary

The one person that is present in every guard company is the secretary or, more appropriately, the administrative assistant, as the demands of a secretary in a guard company go far beyond normal secretarial functions. In many small offices, the secretary is the only administrative staff and must handle all administrative matters for the company.

Normally, a secretary provides administrative support in handling correspondence, reception, filing, and routine clerical tasks. In the guard company, he or she may conduct initial screening of job applicants, conduct background checks, and issue uniforms. Because of the tendency to place many of these tasks on a good secretary, it is important that management define the position clearly to avoid overtasking one person.

Receptionist

A guard company does much of its business over the phone. Clients and potential clients, guards, job applicants, vendors, and a host of others can be expected to call in the course of the day's operations. Although this function is usually combined with the secretarial position in smaller offices, it should be carefully monitored. By tracking the volume and routing of calls, it is possible to determine whether a part-time receptionist might be more cost-effective in the long run than disrupting the secretary's work patterns every time the phone rings. Unanswered phones can result in lost business.

A common problem is that receptionists are usually low-paid, entry-level employees with no knowledge of the company or its operations. This can have disastrous consequences for a company that is in a service industry. If the company chooses to employ a receptionist, he or she should be held to the highest standards of customer service and should receive extensive training and orientation on the company and the guard industry.

Clerical Worker

Much of the work in a guard office is routine paperwork, such as the filing of reports, processing of payroll, and records maintenance. It can be extremely cost-effective to free high-paid administrative staff from these tasks and allow them to focus on more complex problems by hiring an inexpensive clerical. For example, using an operations manager to file routine post reports takes him or her away from the job of developing staffing plans and training dispatchers. Using a dispatcher after hours to do filing can distract the dispatcher from making a required telephonic check on a post.

What normally happens in a guard company is that routine paperwork receives a low priority and does not get done until a crisis occurs. Then it becomes critical to locate a specific report or to reconstruct a customer's bill. A good clerical worker provides continuity and ready access to vital records. If the time spent by management searching for an important file is considered as an expense, a clerical worker becomes even more cost-effective than is shown in the example in Figure 3.1.

Administrative Tasks

Licensing

A guard company is first and foremost a business. As such, it must meet the normal business licensing requirements of the jurisdiction in which it operates. The minimum requirement is usually a city and/or a county business license. This may involve the payment of a licensing fee and the imposition of a gross receipts or payroll tax on the business. Operating without a business license can result in substantial penalties. If the guard company is incorporated, there is usually a requirement to file with the state in which the company operates.

In most states, guard companies have added licensing requirements for both the management of the company and for individual guards. For example, the state of New Jersey requires that the guard company owner meet extensive experience requirements and that each guard submit a fingerprint card to the state police. In California, guard company owners must pass a written test prior to licensing, and each guard must complete a written test and submit a fingerprint card to the Bureau of Collections and Investigations. A good place to check to get general information on various state requirements is the *Security Letter Source Book* published annually by Butterworth-Heinemann.

A major administrative task is the tracking of expiration dates on licensing and permits. In California, for example, each guard is responsible for obtaining his or her own guard permit and for renewing it periodically. The guard company, however, can incur substantial penalties for allowing a guard to work without a valid permit. The guard company must have a system that tracks information regarding the expiration of certifications and licenses and provides this information in a timely fashion.

The most efficient way to establish an information tracking system is through the use of a computerized database program. Many of the scheduling programs developed for use by the guard industry, such as Wells Fargo's

TAGSS (The Automated Guard Scheduling System) or Pinkerton's PARS (Pinkerton Automated Resources System) have these databases linked to the scheduling system. Guard information is entered once in the system for all purposes, such as scheduling, records tracking, and payroll. If registration or licensing is not current, the system will not allow the guard to be scheduled. (For further information on automated systems, see chapter 6, "Operations.")

Insurance

Any business venture incurs risks, but guard companies tend to be more at risk than usual because of the nature of the work performed by guards. When a client hires a guard company, that client transfers a certain amount of liability for the protection of the client's employees and property to the guard company. Failure to perform the contract or negligent action on the part of the guard company's employees create significant risk exposure for the guard company. Consequently, a guard company must be properly insured if it expects to continue in business.

Several events in the early eighties significantly affected guard company liability. First, there was a redefinition by the courts of the doctrine of joint and several liability. Previously, if a person was injured by another, he or she was able to collect damages only from the person who was the proximate cause of the injury. For example, if a person was assaulted in a parking structure patrolled by a contract guard, the proximate cause was held to be the criminal who committed the assault.

Beginning with the case of singer Connie Francis who successfully sued a motel owner for failing to protect her against an assault in her room, the courts expanded the definition of proximate cause to include those who had a duty to prevent a crime. This significantly altered the doctrine of joint and several liability. Traditionally, when two or more parties were sued for an injury, the defendant who caused the most injury was held most liable and had to pay the most damages. However, under the new interpretation of this doctrine, sometimes referred to as the "deep pockets" doctrine, the defendant most able to pay may be found liable for all damages owed the plaintiff, even if the defendant was not the most culpable.

This is extremely significant for the guard company. In the example given above, the person assaulted in the parking structure could sue not only the criminal but also the owner of the structure and the guard company as well. The guard company could well find itself paying the bulk of the civil damages assessed by the court, even if the guard was operating in complete compliance with the contract and the client's instructions.

Of equal significance to the guard industry was the effect of the recession in the late eighties on insurance fees. Prior to 1985, insurance fees for guard companies had remained fairly stable and competitive. As the recession affected the invested premium income of the insurance companies, insurance rates for guard companies soared. Many smaller firms went bankrupt. Others chose to operate without insurance. For the remainder, liability and insurance premiums remain a major expense for the reputable guard company.

General Liability Insurance

The risks incurred by a guard company are primarily covered under a general liability policy. Unlike the standard liability policy of other companies, guard company policies must carry specific coverage for errors and omissions and for care, custody, and control. Errors and omissions coverage protects against actions that the company or its employees did or failed to do that resulted in an injury to a third party. Care, custody, and control covers loss or damage to third-party property.

General liability coverage is based on the level of risk or exposure to liability. For example, an armed guard creates more liability exposure, and insurance coverage premiums would be higher than those for an unarmed guard. An office worker with no field responsibilities would have considerably less risk exposure than an unarmed guard and, in some cases, may not even be charged a premium under the company's policy.

Insurance coverage is usually billed as a percentage of salary by type of employee. The normal way of stating this is as cost per $100 of payroll. Note that insurance premiums are based on payroll, not on receipts. In addition, premium rates should be broken out by type of employee so that the company obtains the lowest possible rate. For example, a company with a small number of armed guards and a large number of unarmed guards should not be charged the armed guard premium for all employees. Figure 3.2 demonstrates the difference between the two methods of calculation.

Additional costs can be saved by self-insuring for a certain percentage of the risk. This is done in the form of a deductible. By calculating the amount of loss that can be accepted by the company, the company can negotiate a reasonable deduction with the insurance carrier and reduce the premium. Losses covered under the deductible are normally reported to the insurance carrier in case any additional liability costs arise from the incident.

Because of concerns over liability, many clients will ask the guard company to provide proof of general liability insurance coverage with a proposal for service. An insurance company experienced in providing coverage for the guard industry will usually provide a certificate of insurance at no charge. Conversely, the insurance carrier may ask to review any contracts accepted by the guard company to determine if there is any potential increase in liability.

CATEGORY OF EMPLOYEE	INSURANCE RATE PER CATEGORY	ANNUAL PAYROLL BY CATEGORY	COMPANY A	COMPANY B	COMPANY C
REGULAR GUARDS	0.038	$936,000	$46,800*	$35,568	$35,568
ARMED GUARDS	0.05	$218,400	$10,920	$10,920	$10,920
OFFICE STAFF	0	$110,000	$5,500*	$4,180#	$0
TOTAL INSURANCE PREMIUM	N/A	N/A	$63,220	$50,668	$46,488
* Billed at armed rate of .05 #Billed at regular guard rate of .038					

Figure 3.2   Insurance rate comparison.

Excess Liability Coverage

Excess liability coverage is designed as special catastrophic coverage that protects against events that exceed the limits of the general liability policy. This coverage may also be referred to as an "umbrella" policy because it covers several smaller policies. While this type of insurance can be relatively inexpensive, it is not always available to guard companies because of the high degree of risk and the large damage amounts traditionally awarded for guard negligence.

If the guard company is large enough to self-insure for the amounts usual for a general liability policy, excess liability provides the additional protection that might be needed in a large lawsuit at a very reasonable cost.

Fidelity Bonds

In the coverage of risk for guard companies, no term is more misunderstood than the word *bond*. A bond refers to a guarantee by the insurance company to cover a particular type of risk. This is normally taken by the public to mean that dishonest acts by the guard will be paid for by the insurance carrier. In actuality, there are several different types of bonds carried by guard companies, and only one will protect the client against dishonest acts by guards.

In some states, there is a requirement to post a *licensing bond*. This pool of money serves mainly to protect the state against being sued for failing to assure proper performance of the company. To obtain relief, the client must involve the state in a lawsuit.

Larger clients may require the guard company to post a *bid bond* when submitting a proposal for service. A bid bond is a monetary guarantee that the guard company will accept and perform the contract for which it is bidding. If the company fails to accept the contract after it is awarded, the bid bond is forfeit, and the funds are used to cover the costs of rebidding the contract. Bid bonds are usually required by public agencies, such as the federal government, and by large corporations. As the amount of the bond can be as much as half the value of the contract, the bid bond represents a significant commitment for the guard company and should be used only when absolutely necessary.

Once a contract is awarded and accepted, some clients require the posting of a *performance bond*. This bond is a guarantee that the company will fulfill the contract in accordance with the agreed upon specifications. If the guard company fails to perform, the bond covers the client's costs in obtaining a new contractor.

When using the term *bond* most clients are thinking of a *fidelity bond*, which protects against the dishonest acts of the contractor's employees. Unfortunately, not all bonds protect third parties. The standard bond used by most businesses protects the business against theft by employees *from the business*. Such a bond would protect the guard company owner if the guard stole from him or her but would not protect the client if the guard stole from the client. Therefore, the guard company that desires or is required to bond employees must be sure that the bond covers third parties as well as the guard company.

Special Insurance Coverage

Depending on the type of duties performed by the guard company, it may be necessary to purchase additional specialized insurance coverage. The most common type of specialized coverage is vehicle insurance.

Guard companies may own, rent, or lease vehicles or may require employees to use their own vehicles or vehicles provided by the client while on company business. Each situation has its own distinct insurance requirements. For example, if an employee uses his or her own vehicle on company business, the company will incur some liability for the employee's actions while operating the vehicle. While the employee will have his or her own insurance policy, that policy may not cover the use of the vehicle in the course of employment. It may be necessary, therefore, for the company to purchase a limited policy that covers this risk.

Vehicle insurance policies usually include coverage that protects against liability for bodily injure to third parties (liability coverage) and coverage that covers damage to the vehicle (comprehensive or collision coverage). By analyzing the coverage provided by these policies against coverage provided by other policies and the ability of the company to self-insure, the guard company can reduce vehicle insurance costs to the absolute minimum.

Forms Management

Guard companies thrive on forms. The average company has a form for any occurrence: timekeeping forms, report forms, inspection forms, uniform issue forms, accident report forms, etc. In addition, guards and supervisors have a tendency to create their own forms to meet specific client needs. With so many forms being generated, the guard company can quickly become overwhelmed and unable to find the information it needs for decision making.

The administrative function needs to control form generation in the company. While it may be permissible to use an "unofficial form" for a specific, one-time event, forms should be developed and approved through a formal process.

The first step to designing a form is to determine if it is really necessary. Can an existing form be used? Does this form replace one already in use? The single most important question to ask is, do we need to collect this information? If the form serves no purpose other than to collect information that "might" be needed, it probably should not be approved. The basic principle of forms management is that a form should be developed only if there is a justified need for it.

Forms in a company should be standardized, both in terms of materials and size, as well as general appearance. By using standard-sized forms (i.e., forms that are based on the standard $8\frac{1}{2}$-by-11-inch or 17-by-22-inch sheet), the company can substantially reduce printing and production costs. For example, sixteen forms measuring $4\frac{1}{4}$ by $5\frac{1}{2}$ inch can be cut from a standard 17-by-22-inch sheet without any waste. The same form, designed as a $4\frac{1}{2}$-by-$5\frac{3}{4}$-inch form, results in only twelve forms per sheet and requires more paper to print the same number of forms than the smaller size.

In designing the form, thought must be given to how the form is going to be used within the company and how to ensure the effective flow of the information gathered on the form to those who need it. For example, if time cards are to be given to a data-entry clerk for entry into a computerized payroll system, the time card should record information in the sequence in which it is entered. This reduces the amount of time the clerk must spend on each form and may mean the difference between using a full-time or part-time clerk.

Forms designers frequently overlook the requirement for multiple copies of forms. The cost of reproducing a completed form on the photocopier may seem insignificant, but the per sheet cost over time exceeds that of printing an additional copy of the form. By the same token, printing numerous copies using expensive carbon manifold paper when only one or two copies are required is a waste.

The introduction of a new form should include provision for storage or disposal of the completed form. For example, time cards and incident reports are legal documents that should be stored for a period of time. An internal message form may contain time critical information that has no value once the event is past. It is important to determine which forms require storage and for how long so as to avoid creating an administrative burden and incurring additional clerical costs.

Forms have a life cycle. Eventually, the company will discard the form in favor of an improved version, or the need for the form will have disappeared. Outdated forms should be withdrawn as soon as possible and disposed of through recycling. This prevents the accumulation of old forms in storage space and prevents confusion.

Records Management

One of the major tasks of the administrative function is the maintenance of a filing system that allows immediate access to all the company's records. Unfortunately, most filing systems seem to grow by default. The company purchases a filing cabinet and begins filing things by alphabetical order or by some general heading, such as "correspondence." Locating a piece of information requires searching a number of folders and trying to guess how the person filing the information was thinking. In addition, many unnecessary documents are filed and kept for years, while important ones are lost or discarded.

Records management begins with the creation of a functional filing system. This system identifies the general broad categories of the files to be kept, each with an assigned identifying number or letter. Within each category is a series of subdivisions, also with discreet number identifiers. The subdivisions are broken down into individual files, also numbered. For example, the broad category "Client Files" can be broken down into specific subdivisions for each client. Within each subdivision is a file for the contract, for incident reports, or for post orders.

The functional file system also describes disposition instructions for disposal of files. For example, client files might be sent to a records storage location or microfilmed after five years. Tax records might be destroyed after the legal holding period is completed. Old post orders might be destroyed when an updated version is issued. Disposition information should be clearly marked on the file label. The key is to clearly identify how long a file is to be kept and to avoid maintaining unnecessary files.

Within the functional filing system, records should follow accepted filing rules and standards. Using a system that is generally accepted and easily accessed makes the location of information much simpler than using a system invented by the company file clerk. The Association of Records Managers and Administrators (ARMA) develops and promotes standards for records management that are used by most businesses.

Records keeping has associated costs. There is, of course, the cost of the clerical staff to maintain the records. There are other costs that are not as readily apparent, such as the cost of furniture and equipment, office space, and supplies. There is also a cost associated with the time it takes to find a piece of critical information and a potential cost of not being able to produce a vital piece of information during litigation.

Certain files may require indexing. This is particularly true of files pertaining to accidents and criminal incidents. There may be a need to accumulate this type of data for the company as a whole and by client site. The need for an index may also be generated by items that require storage in more than one file category. Bear in mind, however, that not every item being filed needs to be indexed.

Although indexing can be done through a manual system, it is more productive to use one of the readily available computerized database systems. This allows a records clerk to determine the location of a specific document in a matter of seconds. It also allows the sorting of information by specific parameters. The database system can be even more flexible if information is entered directly into the system or if a guard-tour-management system is used to record information (see chapter 6). In addition, many companies are moving to a "paperless" office by scanning records onto optical disks, allowing almost instantaneous indexing and retrieval.

Space Management

Office space is seldom cheap, particularly in large metropolitan areas. In addition, there never seems to be enough room to perform all the functions needed by a guard company. Consequently, the administrative function must squeeze every bit of usefulness out of existing space. This means reducing storage space and equipment requirements to the minimum necessary and organizing the office space to create a smooth work flow for the staff.

Guard offices, like most offices, have areas that are accessible to clients and areas that have controlled access. For example, every office has a reception area of some sort for meeting vendors, job applicants, and visitors. Records and equipment storage areas and administrative offices generally require escorted access.

Guard offices, again, like most other companies, have work loops that perform associated functions. One example would be the processing of a job applicant from reception to personnel for hiring to operations for work assignments to logistics for uniform issue. Another is the link between sales, marketing, and operations. By building the office around functional work loops, it is possible to make maximum use of space while increasing worker efficiency.

An additional consideration is the volume of noise generated by an activity and the level of concentration needed by workers. Dispatchers, for example, spend a great deal of time on the phone, and the noise level in an operations room can be high at times. Office equipment, such as copiers and fax machines, can generate noise and a high volume of employee traffic. Wherever possible, noisy functions should be insulated from other functions. For example, fitting phones with headsets and call lights can reduce noise in the operations room. Copiers might be set up in an area used for storage rather than in a work area.

Some office space can serve dual functions. For example, a conference room can also serve as a classroom or as a payroll processing area for part-time staff. A uniform storage area with locking closets and cabinet areas can serve the same function.

Balancing all these factors is difficult, and there will be compromises and trade-offs. However, by focusing on functional work loops and on the flow of work, you can make use of even the smallest space.

4

Marketing and Sales

To survive, any business needs a continuous influx of new customers. It is important, however, to acquire the right type of customer—one who is profitable and who can be expected to remain a customer for a long period of time. To retain a customer, it is necessary to provide the service the customer needs. The process of attracting and retaining the customer is known as *marketing*.

Marketing

Marketing versus Sales

When asked who in the company has the most to do with marketing, most guards will invariably reply that the sales manager does. They make the same mistake that many managers do: they confuse sales with marketing.

A sale is a financial arrangement. The client agrees to purchase the services of a guard company and signs a contract to that effect. The mechanics of this process are usually performed by the company's sales representative. The sale or, as it is more properly known, the closing, is only the final act in a long series of events, the culmination of the process known as marketing. Where a sale is a single act, marketing, in the words of Jay Levinson, "is everything you do to promote your business" (Levinson, 1984, p. 3).

Unlike a manufacturing company that sells a tangible product, the guard company provides a service. Consequently, its focus must be on the consumer, the potential client. All company activities must be fully integrated and focused on gaining and keeping a client through good service. Consequently, the goals and objectives formulated by management must be fully meshed with an integrated market strategy.

Marketing Strategy

Marketing begins with policy decisions by management as to the potential clients desired by the company. Will the company seek to acquire large corporations, municipalities, public agencies, or retail stores as clients? Will the company be a high-end company offering premium-quality service or will it seek market entry by accepting accounts no one else wants? Another way of approaching this is to analyze the company and decide what clients it can best serve.

The image the company will seek to present to potential clients must be consistent with the market sector that is targeted for penetration. For example, the decision to seek corporate clients may determine that the standard guard uniform be a jacket and tie rather than a police style uniform (see chapter 8). The decision to bid on federal government contracts may require the recruitment of guards able to obtain security clearances.

The selection of a target market must be based on a careful analysis of potential clients and an in-depth understanding of the guard company. This analysis seeks to understand the needs of the potential client: how likely the client is to use contract guards, how many, what duties will be performed, etc. The company then examines these client needs in light of its own capabilities. The company is seeking a market in which its abilities will give it a strong competitive advantage over other guard companies. For example, many new guard companies gain entry to the market by accepting low-bid contracts that are too small to attract the attention of larger companies. Large companies, on the other hand, have the resources to bid on larger, more complex contracts.

In analyzing competition, the guard company must also understand *how* it intends to compete. Most guard companies compete on just two variables: price and quality of service. The guard company must determine, therefore, just what its product mix will be. It is possible to structure a contract to provide extremely high-quality premium service but lose out to a competitor with a lower bid. Conversely, a bare-bones contract paying minimum wage may not generate sufficient cash flow to maintain good service or profitability.

This brings up another strategic goal that is often overlooked. It is not sufficient to merely win a contract. The long-term success of a guard company will ultimately depend on how many clients it can retain. Rapid turnover of clients increases costs and disrupts cash flow, making long-term planning difficult. Although a client will always be concerned about price, once the contract is signed the client generally focuses more on quality of service.

This is the reason why company goals and objectives must be fully integrated with marketing strategy. The personnel charged with sales and marketing can attract clients, but it is the smooth coordination of all company functions that produces the quality of service that will retain a client.

Company Image

An inherent part of the company image is the company name. Most guard companies select names that are associated with strength and security, such as "Fortress Security." Others use names that reflect their target client, such as "Corporate Defenders." Still others use the name of the founder and rely on the reputation of that name, for example, "Holmes and Watson Security."

One practice that has come under increasing criticism is the selection of a company name that tends to imply some official sanction. These names usually include the terms bureau, department, special police, agency, or something similar, such as "City of X Private Protection Bureau." Several states have passed laws specifically prohibiting this practice. Such a name projects a negative image—by implying that the company views itself as a quasi-police force—and should be avoided.

Once a name is selected, a company logo and color scheme is the next step. The logo becomes the embodiment of the company image. It should be used on all company documents and forms, in the uniform patches of the guards, and in any advertising. The goal is to build public recognition of the logo. The logo must be easily recognizable and associated with the company. For example, the Burns shield and the Pinkerton eye have immediate public recognition and provide a link in the mind of the public with each agency's colorful history.

With the logo goes a company color scheme. While corporate colors may seem to be the province of big business, it is important for the guard company to present a consistent, coordinated image. This creates an aura of organization and, above all, reliability. In time, the company colors become identified with the company and an extension of its image. Consider the instant recognition afforded to the brown UPS trucks or the blue uniform of the Postal Service. The most obvious way that corporate colors can be applied to the guard company is through the careful coordination of uniform styles (see chapter 8).

Advertising

Guard companies spend millions of dollars each year on advertising. Yet much of that advertising is ineffective because it fails to reach potential clients. This is because a lot of guard advertising uses a shotgun approach without targeting a specific market share.

The key word here is exposure. There must be sufficient advertising to keep the company in the public eye, but at the same time the advertising must reach the desired clients. This involves a careful analysis of the target market. For example, what publications are read by the potential clients? If the company has targeted a specific trade or industry, part of its advertising budget should be allocated for advertising in periodicals specific to that trade or industry. Membership or associate membership in organizations peculiar to the client's business may also be useful. A company specializing in high-rise building security, for example, may choose to belong to the Building Owners' and Managers' Association (BOMA). Active community involvement, such as membership in the Chamber of Commerce or the Better Business Bureau, should also be considered.

To be effective, advertising must answer a specific need in the client's mind. Market analysis should be able to determine what type of guard the target client wants and what duties that guard must be able to perform. The type of guard needed at a nuclear power plant, which faces a risk from a terrorist attack, is not the same type of guard needed to patrol a public school yard. The guard company must be able to project an image that tells the client "I have just the right guard for you." Consequently, brochures and other company literature should be clearly focused on the client and not generic.

Advertising must be consistent and repetitive. A small advertisement repeated regularly in a publication has a better effect than a large one shown only once or twice. This is because consistency leads to familiarity, which in turn breeds customer confidence. While the advertisement may change, the theme and image presented should remain constant.

Marketing Tools

Most guard companies retain a sales representative. Few however, provide the tools necessary for the sales representative to aggressively market the company. Marketing is the essential first step to making the sale, however. The sales representative has to have some means of attracting potential clients. What is more important, they must be the right type of client. A company specializing in protecting corporate offices will not last long if its marketing efforts attract only low-bid contracts. Consequently, the company needs to develop a number of marketing tools consistent with its overall marketing strategy.

Client List

The first tool is a qualified contact list. This seems basic, yet many companies do not take the time to develop a list of potential clients and to analyze the list for likely prospects. The marketing person begins by listing all potential clients, then researches each name on the list thoroughly. The initial list should have been derived during the market study discussed earlier. Other sources include the daily news, organization directories, the telephone book, trade shows, and so forth. For example, a company in San Francisco can readily obtain *The Bay Area Employer Directory*, which lists the names, specialties, number of employees, volume of business, and key officers for almost all major employers in the Bay Area. Also available is the Better Business Bureau's *Consumer Resource Book and Membership Roster*, which is a source for both potential clients and advertising.

The list will be lengthy and many of the companies will not need or want guard services. The marketing person must next qualify the list by finding those companies that might require such services. This is a time-consuming process that may involve telephone surveys, cold calls, and monitoring industry news. The researcher is attempting to identify which companies use guards, whether contract or proprietary, and who is the principal decision maker for purchasing guard services. This decision maker (usually the security manager or director of security) then becomes the target for the marketing effort.

Another category of potential client is the company that does not use guards but probably should. In this case, the sales representative could consider offering a free security survey that points out potential losses and the cost savings of using a guard.

Initial contacts should be low key and informational in nature. For example, if the company uses proprietary guards, have they considered the cost savings in using contract guards? If the potential client has not, the sales representative could offer to do a free analysis. If the company uses contract guards, are they satisfied? Again, a free security survey of the existing force could be offered. When is the current contract up for renewal? If it is in effect for several years, it might be worthwhile to wait before targeting the potential client for a heavy marketing effort.

The key to making the marketing effort work, however, is to develop and maintain a relationship with each potential client. By carefully cultivating this relationship, the marketer personalizes the guard company and begins to build a certain level of client trust. He or she can demonstrate an understanding of the client's firm and its unique needs.

Company Literature

A company is frequently judged by the quality of its literature. Subconsciously, the potential client equates the appearance of the brochure, pamphlet, or business card left by the sales representative with the level of service the client can expect from the company. A professional, well-designed piece of literature indicates a professional, well-run company.

The rule of thumb on company literature is simple: produce a top-level product or don't produce anything. One superb brochure is worth several mediocre ones. Consequently, the company should seek the assistance of a professional graphics artist in the design and layout of company literature. Graphic artists can also design company logos, business cards, letterheads, envelopes, and so forth. The artist can only design the layout, however. What the literature says must be written by the guard company and should be oriented toward the potential client.

The brochure is a standard handout used at client meetings, conventions, and so forth. Many companies also produce sophisticated booklets in 8$\frac{1}{2}$-by-11-inch format to be used with strong prospective clients. Again, the intent is to convey a specific company image to the prospect and convince him or her that the guard company can meet the needs of the client's organization. These expensive pamphlets communicate to the client that he or she is dealing with a substantial company who considers the client important enough to provide the best it has.

Again, content is every bit as important as the layout. The initial image should not only grab the client's attention but also make the client want to read the brochure or pamphlet. The text must then convince him or her that the company should be seriously considered as a solution to the client's security problems. The literature should tell the client why the company is different from others, why it should be the first choice for service. The client should be intrigued enough to want to meet with the sales representative and discuss price.

Sales

Once the client is ready to talk price, the sales representative goes to work to secure a contract. A sophisticated client will generally provide a *request for proposal* (RFP). The RFP contains most of the information needed by the sales representative to develop a formal bid for the client. It also ensures that all qualified bidders compete equally by meeting the same requirements. For example, a good RFP will set the hourly wage for a guard and specify any benefits to be paid. Without this as a starting point, low-bid companies can appear to enter a more effective bid because they are willing to pay guards minimum wage. Because the requirements of the contract are known up front, the client can evaluate all the competing bids against these requirements.

Where the client chooses not to issue an RFP, the sales representative must carefully interview the client to determine the contract requirements.

This includes basic requirements such as the hours of coverage and duties required, uniforms and equipment, site-specific training, and any special employee selection requirements. The sales representative should also work with the client to establish a schedule of wages and benefits. This will allow the representative to educate the client as to acceptable wages for the geographical area.

The basic information provided by the client is then translated into a *contract proposal*. Many sales representatives are experienced enough to do this themselves, but a complex contract requires input from the operations and accounting functions. Operations translates the contract requirements into specific manpower and equipment needs (see chapter 6). The accounting function determines the cost of performance based on the input from operations and computes the rate to be charged to the client (see chapter 7).

The rate is then written into the proposal by the sales representative. The proposal should also contain information on the company, supervisor and management inspections, insurance coverage, and audit and review procedures. Since the proposal will normally become the contract, it is imperative that the sales representative include all pertinent information, particularly with regards to rates and fees. While it is always possible to amend a contract, it is extremely costly to do so and can lead to ill feelings between the company and the client.

Presentation of the proposal is critical. For a simple contract or a small client, a neatly typed proposal and cover letter is acceptable. When bidding on a large contract or dealing with an important client, the proposal becomes another marketing tool. Although the company will probably use a standard form for the proposal or contract, entering this standard form into a computer allows each client to receive a proposal that looks as if it was designed and typed specifically for him or her. This document can then be placed in a folder in the company color and imprinted with the company logo. The other pocket on the folder can be used for company literature, articles on the guard company, comparisons between the proposal and existing services, and so forth.

More elaborate proposals can be placed in three-ring binders or spiral-bound. One company uses a three-ring binder that contains preprinted dividers and pages on company history and management. Specific client data and rates are typed using the same paper stock and typeface and placed in the appropriate sections of the binder to complete the proposal. Spiral binding can also be extremely impressive, particularly when coupled with preprinted covers containing the company logo. Spiral binding can be done by a printer or on an inexpensive desktop machine.

Proposals should be presented in person whenever possible. This allows the sale representative to fully explain the proposal and to answer any questions the client might have. If the guard company is the sole bidder on the contract, the sales representative can resolve any problems on the spot. If other bidders are involved, the sales representative should consider pointing out specific advantages in the proposal that the client should consider when looking at others. These advantages should almost always be oriented toward quality of service. A quality guard company should not have to compete on the basis of price alone.

The Guard Services Contract

The contract is an agreement between the client and the company regarding the work that it is to be performed and the payment for such work. It formalizes the verbal agreements made by both sides during negotiations leading up to acceptance of the proposal. While many companies operate "on a handshake" without a contract, this is a poor management practice. It is difficult to prove that the guard company is complying with the specifications given by the client (contract compliance) or that the client has failed to pay the agreed upon amount (breach of contract) unless there is a written agreement between them. Written contracts are governed by the Uniform Commercial Code and should be prepared and reviewed by the company attorney.

The Basic Contract

The contract provides a certain degree of protection for both parties by providing remedies and penalties for breach of contract. For example, government contracts usually contain substantial penalties for allowing a guard to work over twelve hours in a twenty-four hour period on the theory that his or her performance deteriorates after this time. In addition, the contract clearly defines liability on the part of both the client and the company for theft and loss.

The contract need not be elaborate. For small jobs, a simple letter spelling out terms and signed by the client might be sufficient. When the job is large and a detailed proposal has been submitted, it is not unusual for the proposal itself to constitute the bulk of the contract. The client writes a letter accepting the proposal after all agreed upon changes have been made. This system is usual when dealing with government contracts and large corporations where the amended proposal, commonly known as the *best and final proposal,* constitutes the contract upon acceptance.

While the two forms of contract just discussed are fairly common, most guard companies use a standard contract for almost all clients. For the most part, the contracts are identical for each client, with only specific terms of service and payment changed. This allows the sales manager to "fill in the blanks" quickly without having each contract reviewed by the company attorney. Specific schedules and rates are attached to the basic contract as exhibits.

Any changes or unusual service requests in a standard contract should be reviewed by the company attorney. To be legally binding, the contract should contain at least the following information:

1. identity of the parties to the contract (i.e., the name of the client and the guard company);
2. the subject of the agreement (i.e., what services are to be rendered);
3. time for performance (i.e., the length of time the contract is in force);
4. cost.

Because many companies use standard contracts, most client-specific information is listed as an attachment or exhibit to the basic contract. This attachment should provide detailed information on the scope of the contract. As a minimum, the attachment should contain the following:

1. the location where the work is to be performed;
2. specific hours of coverage;
3. the minimum level of staffing for both guards and supervisors, to include field supervisors;
4. specific duties to be performed by guards and supervisors;
5. required uniforms and equipment, including who will provide;
6. the billing rate for each category of guard and supervisor;
7. special training, certifications, or licensing.

Additional Provisions

In addition to the basic contract, there are a number of other provisions that are commonly found in guard contracts. These are designed to build in various safeguards for both the client and the guard company and are fairly common to most contracts.

Most guard contracts run continuously until canceled, so it is prudent to include provisions for notification of cancellation (usually thirty days written notice by either party) and for an annual adjustment to the price of services.

Guard contracts should clearly state limits of liability for persons or property guarded. If this is not done, the client and the courts may assume that the guard company will indemnify the client for any loss or injury incurred at the site. It is imperative that the guard company state whether or not it will pay for loss and under what circumstances. The same section also addresses any indemnification agreed to by the client and the guard company.

The relationship of security guards to the client should be addressed in the contract. This section should state that the guards are employees of the contractor and spell out any supervisory requirements. This is particularly important where the client is providing on-site supervision. If this section is not clearly thought out, the guard company may be liable for improper instructions given to the guards by client supervisors.

The section on client-guard relationships may also address the client's right to interview guards prior to assignment and to have substandard guards removed from the site. It should also include a clause that precludes the client from hiring guards away from the guard company. This issue usually surfaces after a contract has been terminated, and the client desires to hire the best guards for a proprietary force or to place with a new contractor.

Several other legal clauses are standard in most contracts, including provisions for amending the contract and for recovering attorneys' fees and court costs for any litigation arising from a contractual dispute. There is normally a clause that states that the contract is the sole agreement between the contractor and the client and that all changes must be made in writing and agreed to by both parties. Finally, there are usually clauses regarding the assignment of rights to the contract and stating that if a portion of the contract is found to be invalid, the remaining provisions are still in effect.

Preparing the Contract

Most of the provisions just discussed are standard for each client and can be stated in a preprinted form. A more impressive approach is to maintain the form on a computer disk. When preparing a contract, the staff fills in necessary information and prints out a final contract that looks custom-designed for the client.

Quality Control

Once the client accepts the proposal and a contract is signed, the client becomes part of the guard company's marketing team. Word of mouth recommendations or condemnations carry tremendous weight. Performing well on a small contract can lead to better ones. For this reason, the sales representative must provide a measure of quality control for the guard service. This means maintaining the relationship developed prior to award of the contract and paying periodic visits to the client's site to check on the service. This information can then be fed back to the operations staff or, if necessary, to the company management.

The manager of the guard company must be heavily involved in the marketing effort, beyond developing the goals for the sales representative. Potential clients usually like to know with whom they are dealing and will either request a meeting with the manager or visit the company office. If the client does not, the manager should consider visiting him or her. Whenever possible, the manager or a senior representative should be present when a proposal is presented and the contract signed.

Once the contract is signed, the manager must meet regularly with the client to ensure that service is satisfactory. One national company, for example, requires that a branch manager meet with each client once a month. Another has members of its senior corporate management contact clients periodically in addition to the regular visits required of its branch managers. Frequent client contact can fine-tune service and eliminate potential problems.

Management involvement should be backed up by an aggressive quality-assurance program. This program is usually implemented through field inspection of guards by both supervisors and managers to ensure compliance with the contract and with company standards. The company should have a system in place that ensures that all guards and client sites are inspected on a regular, but unannounced, basis and that records the results of inspections and any corrective action taken. These results should be readily available for client inspection. More information on inspection programs can be found in chapter 10, "Supervision."

The guards themselves are the company's primary marketing tool. Quality of service is noticed not only by the client but by every visitor that enters the client's place of business. For this reason, guards must present the desired image and must be briefed on how to refer requests for service or information about the company. It is critical, therefore, that the guard manager periodically visit the client's site, not only to meet with the client but to take a good, hard look at the guards working there.

Effective marketing and good salesmanship will gain accounts. Ultimately, however, it is quality of service that will retain them.

5

Personnel

Where do guards come from? How does a company find the "right" guard for a particular post? This is the province of the personnel function: to recruit suitable candidates, select those qualified to be guards, and prepare them for duty. But the personnel department provides more than this. In many companies, it is also responsible for training, for administering the company benefits program, for logistics, for the preparation of payroll data—in short, for everything that affects the guard as an individual.

Laws Related to Personnel Management

There are many laws governing employer-employee relations, including federal legislation, state laws, and local ordinances. Federal law focuses primarily on discriminatory practices, while state and local laws deal with specific personnel issues, such as licensing, working hours, and accident claims. The personnel specialist must be familiar with the various labor laws and serve as the company's advisor on such matters.

Civil Rights Legislation

Title VII of the Civil Rights Act of 1964 prohibits discrimination in all aspects of personnel management: hiring, termination, promotion, compensation, and conditions of employment. The Equal Employment Opportunity Commission (EEOC) is the arm of the federal government charged with monitoring compliance with Title VII. Its powers were significantly increased by the Equal Employment Act of 1972. The EEOC has also adopted a set of standards for hiring practices, the *Uniform Guidelines on Employee Selection Procedures*, the most recent revision being adopted in 1978. The *Uniform Guidelines* prohibits any hiring practice or policy that results in a difference in rate of selection or rejection between minority groups or the sexes. This has a direct impact on the use of tests as part of the hiring process.

Title VII does more than prohibit discrimination; it governs practically every aspect of personnel management. For example, Title VII requires that a company keep personnel records and post notices containing provisions from Title VII, as well as information on filing a complaint.

The Occupational Safety and Health Act

The personnel specialist usually has responsibility for ensuring the company's compliance with the Occupational Health and Safety Act (OSHA) of 1970 and related state laws. The Act was promulgated to ensure employee safety in the workplace and poses some unique problems for the security guard company as guards tend to work in a fairly high-risk environment. A good portion of OSHA compliance involves accurate record keeping and employee education. There are also requirements for reporting accidents and illnesses, notifying employees of risks and hazards associated with the job, and complying with industry-specific safety codes.

Generally, the agencies charged with monitoring compliance are willing to provide copies of relevant laws, wall charts, and even free consulting services. For example, CALOSHA, the branch of the state of California administering OSHA laws and regulations, will visit a work site and recommend improvements for compliance without citing any violations found, as long as they are corrected within a reasonable period. Other sources for information include the local public library, legal bookstores, and paid personnel consultants.

Compensation and Benefits Laws

The personnel specialist must also be familiar with state labor codes and laws. Many of these laws have a direct impact on the security industry. For example, laws relating to payment of overtime will have a bearing on guard costs and should be communicated to the operations function. Rules governing lunch periods are another example. The personnel manager must also be familiar with worker compensation laws, which deal with on-the-job injury and are of particular interest to a security company whose employees are exposed to unusual hazards.

The Hiring Process

The hiring of personnel poses several risks for the guard company. First, the costs associated with recruiting, hiring, and training a new guard can be considerable. It is therefore in the best interest of the company that the hiring process be as efficient and cost-effective as possible. Second, if the company's hiring procedure is or appears to be discriminatory, it represents a considerable liability exposure. For this reason, each candidate must be treated exactly the same, and questions regarding age, marital status, race, and so forth must be avoided by interviewers and on application forms. Finally, security companies have a duty to hire personnel who meet certain standards. If a guard commits a criminal act and is found to have a history of such acts, which the guard company should have discovered in the hiring process, the company can be sued for negligent hiring practices.

It is important to note that hiring is a process that consists of a number of procedures. The personnel manager may select any or all of these procedures depending on the type of employee being recruited. To do so, he or she must be aware of the value and shortcomings of each. A common error in hiring in guard companies is to place too much reliance on the personal interview and application and not enough on other procedures, such as polygraph or personality tests.

Obviously, the more procedures used, the more precise will be the process. However, each added procedure increases the cost of hiring a candidate. It is important, therefore, to select procedures appropriate to the type of assignment and level of responsibility of the employee. For example, selecting a candidate for the accounting division might require a different series of procedures than a guard. It is also important to arrange the procedures in order of cost so that the more expensive procedures are accomplished last. An applicant should not be given a polygraph test before being asked to fill out an application. A full background investigation by an outside investigator should not be accomplished before a $15 personality test.

Many companies find it useful to provide each candidate with a printed handout listing the steps of the hiring process and the requirements for being hired. A small percentage of candidates withdraw when they see that the company will be doing background checks or using personality tests.

Recruiting

The first step in the hiring process is to locate suitable candidates. The emphasis is on *suitable* as it is a waste of the personnel specialist's time to interview candidates who by virtue of criminal convictions, drug abuse, alcoholism, etc., would not be acceptable guards. At the same time, the recruiting effort must not be so restrictive that only a few candidates apply.

Information on the type of candidate needed comes from two sources. The first is the salesperson, who must notify the operations and personnel functions of upcoming contracts. The second is the operations function. Operations personnel should be projecting needs based on manpower planning (see chapter 6) and on anticipated losses. They should also have a very clear idea of the type of duties the guard must be expected to perform. This allows the personnel specialist to develop a rough job description for the vacant positions, which should list the duties to be performed and the specific requirements of the position. While this job description may not be as formal as one done in a large corporation, it is just as important. It is the guide that will allow the personnel specialist to determine if a candidate is suitable for hiring.

The job description is an important part of the hiring process. Under the fair hiring practices regulations, the company cannot discriminate on the basis of factors such as age and physical handicap. Consequently, the personnel department must be able to defend such hiring criteria as "age between 21 to 50 years" or "vision correctable to 20/20, capable of hearing normal conversation at ten feet without hearing aid." Even basic criteria such as "functional literacy" or "must be able to speak, read, and write English" can be challenged on the basis of discrimination against certain minority groups. Consequently, the job description must clearly spell out the duties of the position and the reasons for any restrictions.

In addition to the job description, the company may itself develop general hiring standards. Again, these standards must be capable of being defended and must be based on job requirements and accepted industry standards. These minimum qualifications should be spelled out in detail in the company policy manual and should reflect the lowest standards the company is willing to accept, not the ideal. They will apply to all personnel, with additional requirements being added by job descriptions for specific posts. Figure 5.1 lists the minimum standards recommended by the Task Force on Private Security.

The effort required to recruit suitable candidates is a function of the economic climate and the existing labor pool. When jobs are scarce, even guard jobs become desirable. If jobs are plentiful, guard jobs must be made more attractive and competitive. The labor pool from which the guards are drawn is likewise important. Even if many people are seeking jobs, they may not be of the required caliber in terms of education, experience, and so forth. If the personnel specialist is trying to attract only the top candidates, incentives must be offered. This can be done through higher wages, bonuses, benefits packages, etc. Because these incentives must be factored into the contract cost and agreed to by the client, it is critical that the personnel specialist keep the salesperson apprised of the current labor situation and coordinate the incentive packages.

---

1. Minimum age of 18.

2. High school diploma or equivalent written examination.

3. Written examination to determine the ability to understand and perform duties assigned.

4. No record of conviction.

5. Minimum physical standards: a) Armed personnel—vision correctable to 20/20 (Snellen) in each eye and capable of hearing ordinary conversation at a distance of 10 feet with each ear without benefit of hearing aid; b) Others—no physical defects that would hinder job performance.

Figure 5.1 Minimum preemployment screening qualifications from the Task Force on Private Security.

The most common recruiting source is the local newspaper. The advertisement can serve as a screening tool by highlighting the requirements of the job. It can emphasize any special incentives offered. By carefully selecting the publication and section used, the ad can be targeted at a particular portion of the job pool.

There are several things to remember about newspaper advertising. The first is that it is not cheap. The cost will be determined by the size of the advertisement and the frequency of its appearance. Many companies place a standard advertisement on a continuous basis, altering the advertisement as needs change. This can be much more cost-effective than running frequent short-duration advertisements.

The advertisement must be competitive. If the advertisement merely says something like, "Guards wanted—$X an hour" with a telephone number, it will not compete well with the larger advertisements next to it that provide more information. (Unless, of course, the $X is significantly higher than other companies offer!)

Advertisements should be timed to take advantage of the largest possible audience. Most people looking for a job check the Sunday paper. Advertisements run on Sunday and Monday will be more effective than those run on other days of the week. However, if a particular Sunday is on a three-day weekend, the advertisement may be more effective if run later in the week.

While the newspaper is effective, it is not the only source of potential guards. When the labor pool shrinks, the personnel specialist must become more creative. This means posting advertisements in locations where they can be seen by potential guards and conducting preliminary interviews at locations other than the company offices. Unemployment agencies are always willing to cooperate with employers in this regard and may even conduct preliminary screening. Junior colleges offering criminal justice or security courses are potential sources for developing intern programs, as are many vocational schools that offer security training. Seasonal employees or employees who have long periods between jobs, such as teachers, are another possible source.

The Application

The first thing that anyone looking for a job expects to do is fill out an application form. Unfortunately, most companies use standard forms that ask either too much or too little. Forms that ask questions such as age, date of graduation, race, sex, etc., are discriminatory and to be avoided. So too are forms that ask only for address, phone number, and the last three employers, as they do not provide enough information to adequately evaluate the candidate.

The application form does three things: 1) it demonstrates the candidate's ability to read and comprehend instructions; 2) it demonstrates the candidate's ability to write; and 3) it forms the basis of the background check that is part of the hiring process. For these reasons, the application must be thorough without being discriminatory and should be filled out by the candidate in the office. The candidate should not be allowed to take it home and bring it back later. This is to ensure that the applicant can read and write. If the candidate does not have all the information asked for in the application, it can be provided later.

The application should also contain a statement giving permission for the company to verify all information on the application. This statement constitutes permission for other agencies and companies to release information about the candidate. Some companies actually have the candidate fill out and sign form letters addressed to previous employers and references. If a credit check will be part of the screening process, this should also be included in the statement.

The Screening Interview

The purpose of the initial interview is to screen out obviously unqualified candidates. The interviewer should focus on the application, ensuring that all the information is complete and that any explanations given by the candidate are noted on the form. The candidate should be asked general background questions on prior experience and education that might relate to the job. Any factors limiting the candidate's ability to do the job should be discussed.

If the candidate appears unsuitable, he or she should be thanked for their time and told that they will be contacted if a suitable position opens up. The reason for nonselection should be recorded by the interviewer on the application form. This may be needed later if there is ever a complaint about discriminatory hiring practices.

Testing

Depending on the job level for which the candidate is being recruited, testing may be appropriate. There are several types of tests available that deal both with the candidate's honesty and with job skills: skill tests, personality trait tests, and general ability tests. Tests are an extremely effective way to screen candidates. Empirical studies conducted by the American Psychological Association and the United States government have demonstrated that they are objective, nondiscriminatory, and accurate predictors of job performance.

Skills Test

A skills test is fairly easy to develop and justify. A good example is a typing test given to a secretary whose duties include typing. It is important that the test be job-related, however. Skills tests must have content validity as defined by the U.S. government's Fair Hiring Practices. The company must be able to demonstrate that the test measures skills that will actually be used on the job. Validation can be performed by an independent consultant or a testing firm. A typing test given to a secretarial candidate whose duties do not include typing can be challenged. A secretary tested on a manual typewriter can legitimately object to the test if the job description requires the use of a word processor.

Polygraph Testing

The honesty or integrity test is a much more difficult area with which to deal. Federal legislation in the late 1980s severely restricted the use of the polygraph, which had been an accepted industry tool. The legislation did specifically exempt the guard industry, thanks to lobbying by the American Society for Industrial Security, but many states have more restrictive statutes that ban the use of the polygraph.

While use of the polygraph has decreased significantly as a result of the Employee Polygraph Protection Act of 1988, many organizations, including the federal government, continue to use the polygraph as both a screening and an investigative tool. One of the largest guard companies in the United States, Guardsmark, has continued to use the polygraph with excellent results. Specialty guard companies, such as those in the jewelry or pharmaceutical industries, also make extensive use of the polygraph.

The effectiveness of the polygraph is directly related to the skill of the operator. Most laymen believe that the operator hooks the candidate up to the instrument, asks a series of questions, and then determines whether the candidate is lying. They fail to understand that the actual test is only the culmination of a carefully orchestrated process.

A professional polygraphist begins by working with the client to develop the questions that will be asked of the candidate. The questions must be carefully phrased to elicit the information that the client is seeking. The polygraphist then reviews the questions with the candidate in a personal interview. A skilled polygraphist can frequently obtain admissions of wrongdoing or questionable activities during this interview. Because of the "threat" of the upcoming polygraph test, the candidate is under pressure to be honest with the interviewer.

Once the interview is completed and the candidate is comfortable with the questions that will be asked, the polygraph test is conducted. The polygraphist may run through the questions several times, mixing them with innocuous control questions. The polygraphist then reviews the tape and looks for evidence of stress. A reputable polygraphist will never say that a candidate is lying, only that the candidate appears troubled by certain questions or that the client should pursue certain areas during a background check on the candidate.

The polygraph has proven to be an effective screening tool. However, the high degree of negative press generated by its use must be taken into consideration. The poor image of the polygraph is a direct result of the many unskilled polygraphists in the security industry. If the polygraph is selected as a part of the hiring process, the guard company must closely examine the credentials of any polygraphist it selects. The polygraphist should, at a minimum, have had extensive training and experience with the instrument, not just a quick six-week course. He or she should also be a member of the American Polygraph Association and come well supplied with references from other security practitioners.

Personality Trait Tests

The ban on the polygraph caused renewed emphasis on personality trait tests. These tests can be used to either select candidates with desirable qualities, such as a high probability of long-term retention, or screen out candidates who have undesirable traits, such as dishonesty. A recent study by the American Psychological Association (APA) concluded that these tests are useful in identifying dishonesty and in avoiding negligent hiring claims (King & Dunston, 1992, p. 61).

Personality trait tests have been challenged on occasion as being discriminatory under the Civil Rights Act of 1964 and the EEOC's *Uniform Guidelines.* Most recently, Target Stores in California was sued because a candidate objected to certain questions asked on the test given to him when he applied for a security position. In most cases, however, personality trait tests have been found to be nondiscriminatory, a fact that was bolstered by the APA study.

The key to avoiding discrimination claims lies in test validation. *Validity* is a key concept in psychological testing and can be derived in three ways according to the U.S. government's Fair Hiring Practices. A test is said to have *construct validity* if it can be shown to measure personal characteristics that are related to job performance. A test having *content validity* tests skills that will be used in performing the job. *Criterion validity* refers to the relationship between the test and predicted performance. To be legally defensible, the user must be able to demonstrate that a test meets one of these criteria. In the case of the personality trait test, the test must have criterion validity.

Reputable testing companies, such as the Stanton Corporation or John E. Reid & Associates, have conducted extensive validation studies and make these readily available to their clients. They can also conduct local validity studies, if necessary.

Use of Tests

Testing can be used to either eliminate candidates from further consideration or place candidates once hired. For example, a candidate with dishonest tendencies is clearly unsuitable for guard work. A candidate who meets other qualifications but tests as unsuitable for extensive public contact may be just the right candidate for the night shift at a construction site.

Personality trait tests are becoming the norm in the guard industry. The data accumulated by the APA demonstrates that a carefully constructed and validated test does work and is defensible under EEOC guidelines. The low cost of such tests (approximately $15 per test) makes it a reasonable option for even small guard companies.

Consideration should be given to skill tests as well. These can be fairly easily constructed. For example, one California guard company requires that a candidate take the state-mandated guard-licensing test regardless of whether the candidate is already licensed or not. The candidate must also complete an open-book test on the company policy manual. These two tests demonstrate the candidate's ability to read and comprehend written material and his or her knowledge of state laws pertinent to guard operations. By using the state test required of all guards, the company is on strong ground for eliminating from further consideration any candidate who fails the test.

Medical Screening

Depending on the nature of the job, many companies require a physical examination of the applicant by a company physician. The exam is usually to determine if the employee is physically capable of performing the job and if there is a previous medical history that might affect future performance. For example, a candidate with a history of workers' compensation claims may be likely to file a claim against the guard company and might not be a desirable candidate.

Physical examinations, however, are expensive and have come under a great deal of criticism lately as being unnecessary and discriminatory. As a general rule, they should not be used unless the guard company can show a need for the examination.

One medical test that is fairly common, however, is screening for the use of drugs. The Drug Free Workplace Act of 1988 requires employers doing business with the federal government to actively discourage the use of drugs at places of business and has led to a general acceptance of drug testing. While it is controversial and opposed by civil liberties organizations, drug screening can be an effective means of discouraging drug users from applying for guard positions. Because of the nature of security duties, it is fairly easy to demonstrate the need for this type of test, and the cost is minimal. Like all employment screening programs, however, a drug testing program must be researched and thought out prior to implementation and carefully explained in company policy documents.

Another controversial area is the testing of candidates for Acquired Immune Deficiency Syndrome (AIDS). The general intent of such testing is to avoid any strain on the company health care plan. However, the test identifies only the presence of the virus that causes AIDS and not the disease itself. Consequently, it does not reflect the potential performance of the candidate on the job and is not an effective employment screening procedure. Several states have passed legislation prohibiting or limiting the use of AIDS testing, and recent court decisions make it likely that AIDS will soon be considered a handicap under the Rehabilitation Act of 1973.

Background Screening

With few exceptions, most guard companies tend to do little or no background screening on applicants. Many rely on state programs that require the submission of an applicant's fingerprints as the only screen for criminal activity. Until the state completes such a check, the guard is usually allowed to work. Reliance on such a system creates a considerable liability exposure when one considers that twenty percent of the applications for guard certificates in the state of California are rejected each year because of prior criminal convictions (Behar, 1992, p. 46).

Background checks on applicants are labor-intensive. There is no substitute for direct contact, either by phone or in person, when conducting a background investigation. However, a full background investigation may not be cost-effective for every applicant. The personnel specialist, therefore, should set some parameters for the level of check to be performed and indicators for additional investigation. For example, the check for a manager should be more detailed and intense than that for a guard. The discovery of a false piece of information on an application may require further investigation to determine if it was a simple error or an attempt to conceal information. It might also trigger rejection of the applicant without further investigation.

There are a number of screening options available to the personnel specialist. One method is to have an applicant complete several form letters to schools, references, and previous employers during the application process. These letters require the completion of a checklist and are mailed with a return envelope. The guard's personnel record is flagged until the letters are returned. This can require an inordinate amount of time, does not provide immediate information, and can require intensive filing and records management.

A second method is to identify a member of the company who, on a full- or part-time basis, makes a series of phone calls to check each applicant's record. Only basic information is checked and follow-up letters are mailed only when necessary. This provides immediate information on the guard but is extremely labor-intensive.

The personnel specialist should also consider using an independent contractor to perform background checks. There are a number of database services that can provide basic checks for a nominal fee. While not all information is available in all states and some information may not be current, there is a rapid turnaround on requests. These databases are particularly useful when used by an investigator who specializes in background checks. While these services add a cost to hiring a guard, they can be extremely cost-effective when compared to a suit for negligent hiring.

Background checks should include the following:

1. *Criminal records check.* This is the most important piece of information about an applicant, and yet it is the most difficult to obtain. If a state certification system exists, it might be possible to recruit for guards who have already passed a state screening. Some states permit the police to issue a letter to the applicant stating that he or she has a clean record. Some jurisdictions will provide the information by phone; others require a personal visit and signed authorization. In some jurisdictions, it may not be possible to do a criminal record check.

2. *Employment history.* This is fairly easy to check by phone, although many personnel departments will not provide anything beyond basic information, such as dates of employment and position. However, they will sometimes state whether the applicant is eligible for rehire or if the applicant was terminated for cause, or verify data, such as a social security number.

3. *Medical history.* A check of an applicant's medical history provides two things: it determines if the applicant is fit for the job, and it identifies applicants that have excessive workers' compensation insurance claims. Depending on the level of responsibility of the candidate, a physical examination may be appropriate and may include drug screening.

4. *Educational history.* Again, this information can usually be obtained easily over the phone. Level of education may only be important, however, for certain managerial or technical positions.

5. *Credit history.* This is obtained through a credit bureau. Collateral information is usually given on credit reports, and it is possible sometimes to identify employers that were not listed or multiple social security numbers. Recently, credit checks have been challenged on the basis that an individual's credit history does not have any bearing on job performance. The guard company must be prepared to demonstrate that such information is relevant and necessary if faced with an EEOC complaint. There are also very specific requirements regarding obtaining permission from candidates and informing them of the results.

6. *Citizenship status.* This is normally done through documents provided by the applicant as prescribed by law. While there is generally no requirement that a guard be a U.S. citizen, noncitizens must have permission to work in the United States.

Final Interviews and Job Offer

After all steps in the application process have been completed, the candidate's record is reviewed and a determination made regarding hiring. There is usually a final personnel interview, during which the candidate is allowed to review his or her file and answer any questions the personnel specialist may have. Following this interview, the candidate may be asked to interview with the operations section and/or the client to whose site the candidate will be assigned. After completing all interviews, the candidate receives a firm job offer, usually from the personnel section.

The job offer to the candidate should be very specific as to duties, assignments, and salary. To preclude any future confusion over the terms of the offer, it is advisable to give the candidate a written notice of the offer. This process can be simplified with a word-processing computer program. Most guards are hired at the same initial salary level and with similar duties. A form letter offering a position is therefore very easy to produce.

Performance Appraisals

As part of its fair employment practices, the guard company must consider all employees fairly for promotion and salary increases. This implies that there must be a fair method for distinguishing between the substandard and the exceptional employee. As in hiring and termination, an informal system of evaluating a guard's performance can result in charges of favoritism and discrimination. Consequently, it is important that the guard company develop a formal system of employee performance appraisal and use this system as the basis of any personnel actions.

To be effective, a performance appraisal system must be viewed by all levels of the guard company as fair and consistent. This is accomplished by careful monitoring of the appraisals by the personnel department and by the consistent use of the appraisals in decision making. Supervisors must also be trained in the preparation of performance appraisals and be evaluated on how well they perform this important function.

Performance appraisals must reflect specific job responsibilities. This means that the employee is evaluated on how well he or she performs assigned tasks and not on a set of vague personality traits, such as "leadership" or "cheerfulness." In an ideal system, the supervisor and the employee would agree at the beginning of the performance period as to what the assigned tasks will be. While this is not always possible, constant communication between the supervisor and the employee must be encouraged, so that the actual appraisal does not come as a surprise to the employee.

There is a tendency in appraisals to use only numbers in rating job performance. Numbers are viewed as impartial and can be easily summarized and evaluated. The problem is that numbers do not have any inherent justification. The supervisor makes a judgment in assigning numbers and does not have to explain his or her reasons for the rating. While numbers have their place on a performance appraisal, the appraisal should also include a comment section that must be completed by the supervisor. Company policy should mandate that excessively high or low scores be justified in the comment block.

Employees must be given the opportunity to review the performance appraisal and to comment on it. Secret appraisals defeat the purpose of having a performance appraisal system because employees cannot judge whether the system is fair and consistent. If the employee disagrees with the evaluation, there should be a mechanism for allowing the employee to include that disagreement with the appraisal and for a formal review of both sides by senior management.

Disciplinary Actions and Termination

No matter how well a company is run, no matter how well candidates are screened, there will always be employees who, for one reason or another, require disciplining or even termination. With the increase in wrongful discharge suits and discrimination complaints, it is necessary for the guard company to put in place a system of graduated discipline and to ensure that such a system is administered fairly.

The Cost of Terminations

Traditionally, common-law doctrine has held that an employee can be terminated at will and has no particular rights to a job. Recent court decisions, however, have held that where an employer has provided either verbal or written assurances of continued employment to the employee, these rights exist. Consequently, a policy stating that employees are terminated only for "just cause" would be sufficient to invoke these rights under contract law.

An employer can also be held liable under tort law if he or she intentionally inflicts severe emotional distress on an employee or allows harassment by other employees to force quitting. Using the results of a false or poorly administered performance appraisal can also provide grounds for a wrongful discharge suit.

Wrongful discharge suits can be expensive. Between 1982 and 1986, over seventy percent of the wrongful discharge cases in the state of California were won by employees. The average award for each case was $652,100, and punitive damages (damages awarded by the court to "punish" the employer and generally not paid by insurance carriers) averaged $494,000 (Ledvinka & Scarpello, 1991, p. 315).

A smaller cost associated with an improperly handled termination is the cost of unemployment insurance. Unemployment insurance is an employer-borne expense charged on the basis of payroll. Although the rate varies from state to state, the federal maximum is 5.4 percent. The state establishes a reserve account for each employer that is used as a measure of how unemployment claims against the employer relate to the employer's contributions. If the employer's turnover rate is high, the account reflects a low or negative balance, and the maximum rate is charged to the employer. If the employer's turnover rate is low, the account has a large balance, and a lower rate is charged by the state.

Unemployment benefits can be denied to a person if he or she quit voluntarily or was fired for cause. They can also be denied if the applicant refuses a suitable assignment or makes fraudulent claims on the application for benefits. To deny benefits and preserve the reserve account, the employer must be able to prove that one of these conditions exist.

It is in the company's interest, therefore, to establish a system for disciplinary actions and terminations. Because of the complexity of these issues, all terminations should be handled by the personnel manager.

Disciplinary Systems

In developing a disciplinary system, it is important to balance the need for a formal program against the need for flexibility in dealing with each employee. On the whole, it is easier to defend a formal system in court than to defend an arbitrary system. However, a formal disciplinary system that is not carefully administered can be a double-edged sword because of technicalities and the need for maintaining written records. For this reason, all disciplinary actions should be reviewed by the personnel manager.

Many of the components of a progressive disciplinary system have been discussed in the section on policy and procedure in chapter 2, "Management." There must be specific rules, related to the job, which are communicated to all employees and consistently enforced. Violations of the rules should have specific punishments associated with them, and the punishment should fit the crime. This does not necessarily mean the development of lists of punishments and offenses. It should, however, describe the types of punishment used by the company and provide examples of how they might be used. Further, certain offenses, such as theft of client or company property, should be punished by immediate termination. These offenses should be clearly identified. Levels of punishment common to guard companies in order of magnitude are verbal reprimand, written reprimand, suspension, and termination.

Once a violation has occurred, it should be promptly investigated. This investigation must include a discussion with the employee regarding the offense. The disciplinary action, even if it is just a verbal reprimand, must be documented. This documentation must include the violation and the disciplinary action taken.

An important part of the disciplinary system is the inclusion of an appeals process. This is particularly important in dealing with unions. Once the punishment has been determined, the employee should be advised of the appeals procedure and given the opportunity to appeal the punishment before it is imposed.

Terminations

Just as hiring is a process, so also is a termination. The guard company should have a set way of handling terminations that is followed in each case as closely as possible.

Prior to actual termination, there should be a formal review of the circumstances surrounding the termination and of the employee's records. This ensures that sufficient grounds for termination exist and that the dismissal is consistent with company policy and custom. Terminations are normally the result of misconduct (such as committing an offense on the immediate termination list or repeated offenses that have caused activation of the progressive discipline system), poor performance, or the elimination of the employee's job. If a termination does not fall within one of these categories, it should be scrutinized very carefully as the employee may well have grounds for a lawsuit.

The review should also determine if sufficient documentation is available in the employee's file to support the termination. For example, if the termination is the result of progressive discipline, there should be a number of previous actions in the file that substantiate this claim. Poor documentation of the reason for termination is the main reason lawsuits and unemployment protests are lost by employers.

Wherever possible, the employee should have a termination interview with the personnel manager. The manager tells the employee the reason for termination and explains any payments still due to the employee, such as vacation pay. It is a good idea to provide this information in a formal termination letter, so that there will be no question as to what is being agreed to by the company. The letter should also state what responsibilities the employee has regarding the return of company property. A copy of this letter then becomes a permanent part of the employee's file.

Bear in mind that any termination can be the cause of action in a wrongful discharge suit or in a discrimination complaint. A well-conducted and documented termination is a shield against such spurious claims and can result in a decrease in unemployment insurance costs. For this reason, terminations should receive a considerable amount of management attention.

Dispute Resolution

Union contracts generally establish a formal process for resolving disputes between the employee and the company. This process may begin with line supervisors and may end with an impartial outside arbitrator. The purposes of this process are to defuse and resolve issues before they become major problems and to allow the employee to feel that he or she will be heard in a legitimate dispute with management.

Since most guard companies are not unionized, they rely instead on an informal system of dispute resolution. This usually involves working a problem through the supervisory chain until it reaches senior levels of the company. This informal system is usually supplemented with an "open-door" policy on the part of senior management.

For the most part, the informal system of dispute resolution works well. However, as with other aspects of personnel management in guard companies, it needs to be balanced against the advantages of a formal system. This normally involves no more than communicating the system to employees in the form of company policy. Managers have been blindsided by major personnel problems because employees did not feel they had access to senior management and were not aware of open-door policies. A company that has this problem is usually ripe for unionization.

Some guard companies have established a formal dispute resolution system, to include use of an impartial arbitrator, as part of a commitment to their employees. Others have made use of a toll-free number that provides information directly to senior management. The actual cost of such measures are minimal compared to the benefits that they can produce. At a minimum, however, the dispute resolution process in the company must be clearly communicated to each employee.

6

Operations

The operations function is supported by all other functions in the guard company. For example, operations provides manpower requirements to personnel for recruitment. Equipment requirements developed by operations are met by the logistics function. Accounting uses the information provided by operations to generate billing and payroll. Deficiencies noted by operations during inspections are referred to the training function for correction. It is in support of operations that the guard force manager's responsibility for coordination of functions within the company becomes most critical.

Manpower Planning

A basic question that must be answered by the operations staff is, How many guards do we need? The question is not as simple as it first appears. This is because the answer that is being sought is not only relevant to a single, specific site but also to the organization's entire operation.

Consider a single guard post requiring 24-hour coverage. The total hours covered per week would be 168 (24 hours × 7 days) or 8,736 hours per year. By dividing the standard 40-hour shift into the 168 hours of coverage, it appears that only four guards are needed with 8 hours left to be covered either through overtime or by a floating guard, giving a factor of 4.2 for the post. It appears logical to assume that this is the number of officers needed for the post.

However, such an assumption fails to take into account the various factors that affect the guard's availability. There are 2,080 working hours per

Working Hours		
per Year	40 hours per week x 52 weeks	2080
Vacation	40 hours	40
Sick Days	16 hours per month x 12 months	192
Training	16 hours	16
Holidays	8 hours x 5 days	40
Actual Availability		**1792**

Figure 6.1 Availability computation.

year (40 hours per week × 52 weeks). However, this number must be reduced by any hours that the guard is not available for work. For example, assume that each guard is entitled to one week of vacation each year, a total of 40 hours. In this hypothetical case, company policy permits a maximum of two sick days a month, for a total of 192 hours annually. The company also requires 16 hours of specialized training each year, as recommended by *NFPA No. 601, Recommendations for Guard Service in Fire Loss Prevention.* The company also grants five holidays per year, for a total of 40 hours. By adding all these hours and deducting the total from the maximum available hours, the actual availability of each guard is only 1,792 hours per year (see Figure 6.1).

By dividing the total post coverage of 8,736 hours per year by the actual availability of the guards, the post staffing factor now becomes 4.7 instead of 4.2. To meet the requirements for this particular post, the company will need 4.7 guards. This figure will, of course, vary based on the terms of the contract or company policy.

By adding the factors for various contracts, the operations manager can derive a projection for the total number of personnel that should be budgeted for annually by the company. It is unlikely that this number of guards will ever actually be employed by the company. However, this projection provides a goal for the personnel department for recruitment. The closer the personnel count comes to this figure, the more efficiently the company will be operating. When compared with actual performance data, the annual projection can also be used to determine how close to budget a particular contract is running.

Scheduling

Manpower planning focuses on the big picture in a guard force operation, which means total hours and personnel requirements. Scheduling is a more precise discipline; it focuses on determining the actual staffing for each single post. It is the function of the scheduler to translate contract requirements into actual operational terms.

Shift Planning

A contract will generally specify only basic requirements, such as total hours or total hours per post. Figure 6.2 is an example of the coverage requirements from a sample contract. Each post is shown with the total hours of coverage required per day. The scheduler must work with these requirements and determine how many full- and part-time guards are necessary. The goal of scheduling is to meet contractual requirements with the minimum number of guards and the least overtime cost possible.

The scheduler must also consider constraints such as a limit on the hours a guard may work. For example, twelve hours is generally considered the maximum a guard should work without relief in order to maintain alertness. The better guard companies impose this limit as a company policy; government contracts usually mandate it. Another consideration is company overtime policy. Many companies refuse to run overtime unless absolutely necessary and, in order to achieve a more competitive bid price, neglect to build it into the rate charged to the client.

As an example of how the scheduler works, consider the basic twenty-four-hour, seven-day a week post (generally abbreviated 1-24-7 in contract shorthand—one guard, twenty-four hours, seven days). Four guards are re-

LOCATION	DAYS COVERED	HOURS COVERED	TOTAL GUARD HOURS
Supervisor	M-F	0800-1600	40
Post #1 Main Lobby	All	0001-2400	168
Post #2 Main Lobby	M-F	0800-2400	80
Post #3 Loading Dock	M-F	0800-1600	40
Post #4 Loading Dock	M-F	0800-1600	40
Post #5 Patrol	All	0001-2400	168
TOTAL			536

Figure 6.2 Scope of work.

quired to meet this post requirement, with eight hours left over. The scheduler has several options:

1. combine this post with other post requirements and use a *floating guard;*
2. plan for eight hours of overtime for one guard; or
3. rotate eight hours of overtime among the four guards.

Each solution has advantages and disadvantages. The floating guard is more cost-effective in that no overtime costs are incurred. However, this guard is required to learn the duties at five different posts—simple enough if they are at the same facility with similar duties but difficult if they are at different sites. In addition, because the guard is only present at the post one day a week, he or she will not be as knowledgeable about the post as a regular guard. The ideal floating guard is an exceptional employee who is flexible and able to learn quickly. Unfortunately, this type of employee is usually promoted rapidly or assigned to an important account, requiring the location and training of a replacement. The typical floating guard, as opposed to the ideal, is generally a new employee who has not yet been assigned to a full-time post—the worst possible choice. Consequently, this option should be used only at large facilities where posts are similar in nature.

If the company has not planned for overtime in its bid (see chapter 7), the other two options will be an additional expense. For this reason, they are not generally used by most guard companies. This is a very shortsighted approach. The guards that work the post on a regular basis are the most knowledgeable replacements available. In addition, most guards are eager for the extra overtime pay. Training costs for an additional guard are nonexistent, and the client will not have to deal with any unfamiliar faces. In most cases, the guard company that budgets for and uses overtime to cover the extra 8 hours in a 1-24-7 post will provide better coverage.

If overtime is decided upon, the choice between giving it to one guard and rotating it is fairly simple. Some clients prefer to have the senior guard (usually the day-shift guard) work the extra shift. If this option is not chosen, the shift should be rotated. This prevents burning out one guard and building resentment in the others who are not receiving the extra pay.

Shift Rotation

Once the basic and overtime coverage is decided upon, the scheduler begins to develop the actual shifts. Generally, the day-shift guard is the lead or senior guard on the shift because he or she will have the most direct day-to-day contact with the client. Consequently, this shift is developed

SHIFT	SUN	MON	TUE	WED	THU	FRI	SAT
0001-0800	C	C	C	D	D	C	C
0800-1600	D	A	A	A	A	A	E
1600-2400	B	D	D	B	B	B	B

Figure 6.3 Standard shift rotation.

first, and the others are built around it. Figure 6.3 shows the standard schedule used by most guard companies. Note that three guards have the same hours each day they work, while the fourth provides coverage on days the other guards are off duty. The fifth guard is a floating guard who also works at other accounts. This floating guard may either work a standard shift (i.e., the same time every day), relief shifts similar to those the fourth guard covers, or variable shifts that depend on the dispatcher's needs. Also note that each guard has two days off in a row. While this is not necessarily required, it provides the guard with an adequate rest period and is highly desirable.

The relief shift (shift D) under this standard schedule is difficult, and few guards stay on it long. It requires almost constant disruption of sleep patterns with no possibility of adaptation. In addition, the guard needs to learn the duties of each shift, which can vary greatly. An exceptional employee is called for on this shift. Like the floating guard job, however, this shift is usually given to new employees. While this shift is common in the guard industry, it should only be used when absolutely necessary.

Note that the rotation ends with the midnight shift. This provides the guard with adequate rest between shifts. Clinical researchers have demonstrated (Sullivan, 1991, p. 22) that the day-evening-night progression is more easily adapted to by the body's circadian rhythm than the day-night-evening progression typical of many schedules.

The relief shift and coverage of the eight hours of overtime through a floating guard are common in the guard industry because they are obvious, logical solutions. Unfortunately, they do not take into account the limitations of the guards and the physical stress a shift such as the relief shift can create. They are the sign of relatively unsophisticated scheduling.

To eliminate the need for the brutal relief shift and to rotate the eight hours of overtime, the scheduler must look beyond the single week's shift and see long-term patterns. One technique is to "wobble" guards between two shifts. Figure 6.4 is an example of such a rotation. Note that there is one day-shift guard, one night-shift guard, one guard who does both day and swing shifts, and one guard who does both swing and night shift. Each guard has two days off in a row, except for one week in four when the guard works eight

SHIFT	SUN	MON	TUE	WED	THU	FRI	SAT
0001-0800	D	D	D	B	D	D	D
0800-1600	C	A	A	A	A	A	C
1600-2400	B	C	C	C	B	B	B
0001-0800	D	D	B	B	D	D	D
0800-1600	C	A	A	A	A	A	C
1600-2400	B	C	C	C	B	B	B
0001-0800	D	D	D	B	B	D	D
0800-1600	C	A	A	A	A	A	A
1600-2400	B	C	C	C	C	B	B
0001-0800	D	D	D	B	B	D	D
0800-1600	C	A	A	A	A	A	C
1600-2400	B	C	C	C	C	B	B

Figure 6.4   "Wobble" shift rotation.

hours of overtime. Each guard receives a minimum of twenty-four hours off between shifts.

The shift rotation shown in Figure 6.4 is not a panacea. There is the potential for confusion and missed shifts if the schedules are not made clear to the guards. However, this type of rotation balances the need for post coverage with the physical needs of the guards and has very clear advantages over the typical schedule:

1. posts are covered by guards specifically trained for the site;
2. all guards used are familiar to the client;
3. overtime is equitably distributed; and
4. guards are provided with adequate rest periods.

Because of these advantages, this type of rotation should be the first choice for schedulers.

One more note on shift rotations. For large contracts, there is sometimes a requirement to rotate entire shifts, much as a police force routinely does. This does not produce much of a problem as long as the scheduler does not plan for too frequent a rotation. Too-frequent rotations are a bad idea for two reasons: First, the guards will require a certain amount of time to adapt to new duties. Even if the post is the same location, the activities and duties associated with that post can vary substantially between the day and night shifts. Second, the guards will need time to physically adjust to the time changes. The longer the interval between rotations, the better the body will adjust to the change. Frequent rotations can induce stress and fatigue that can severely degrade a guard's performance. For this reason, shift rotations should not be more frequent than every three months. In addition, the shift rotation should maintain the day-evening-night sequence discussed earlier.

Planning for Multiple Posts

The examples just cited looked at a relatively simple post—the standard 1-24-7 post. As contracts expand, the scheduling may become more complex, yet in some ways easier. The more posts and guards involved, the greater flexibility the scheduler has in building schedules. The need for the "wobbling" shift in Figure 6.4, for example, may be eliminated through the use of floating guards who work set shifts. Posts requiring less than twenty-four-hour coverage are usually manageable without rotation or overtime. Where a post is an odd number of hours, such as a truck gate requiring nine hours a day for five days (1-9-5), it is often more productive to plan for the payment of five hours of overtime to the same guard than to attempt to use part-time guards for such a limited period. Shifts exceeding the maximum of twelve hours, however, should be broken into smaller shifts. The key to scheduling is to be creative, reducing the number of guards to the minimum needed to provide the necessary post coverage while giving full consideration

POST	SUN	MON	TUE	WED	THU	FRI	SAT
SHIFT 0001-0800							
Lobby	E	E	E	C	C	E	E
Patrol	M	L	L	L	L	L	M
SHIFT 0800-1600							
Supervisor	--	A	A	A	A	A	--
Lobby	D	B	B	B	B	B	I
Lobby	--	F	F	F	F	F	--
Loading Dock	--	O	O	O	O	O	--
Loading Dock	--	N	N	N	N	N	--
Patrol	M	L	L	L	L	L	M
SHIFT 1600-2400							
Lobby	C	C	D	D	D	D	C
Lobby	--	H	H	H	H	H	--
Patrol	J	J	K	K	K	K	K

Figure 6.5 Multipost schedule based on scope of work in Figure 6.2.

SHIFT	SUN	MON	TUES	WED	THU	FRI	SAT
2330-0830	C	C	C	D	D	C	C
0730-1630	D	A	A	A	A	A	D
1530-0030	B	D	D	B	B	B	B

Figure 6.6   Overlap schedule.

to their physical well-being. Figure 6.5 is an example of a multipost schedule based on the scope of work shown in Figure 6.2.

Not only is creative scheduling beneficial to the company, it actually provides more flexible, better coverage for the client. One technique that is seldom used is the overlapping of guard shifts during peak periods. While it involves a bit more work for the scheduler, this technique can provide additional coverage when the post is busiest. This can be done through the use of unpaid lunch breaks. With an unpaid lunch hour mid-way through an eight-hour shift, the guard is on site for nine hours. While there will be a need for the guard to be relieved for this lunch break, this allows for an overlap with the incoming shift. This is particularly applicable to personnel gates, which require only light coverage during the work day but can become backlogged during shift change. Figure 6.6 is an example of this type of schedule. In using this type of shift, it is important to remember that the guard must be relieved for the lunch period and cannot be expected to work, except in an emergency. If the guard does work through the lunch period, he or she must be compensated in order to comply with labor laws.

The scheduler should also give thought to shift change times. The traditional change at 7 a.m. or 8 a.m. may not always be appropriate. Guards cannot be expected to perform their duties well if they are in the middle of a shift change during the busiest period of the day. Shift changes should take place during the periods of least activity at the post.

Dispatching

Role of the Dispatcher

Where manpower planning deals with the development of the needs and costs associated with staffing a guard operation, and scheduling is concerned with developing a plan based on those needs, the dispatching function focuses on placing the guard on the site. It is the difference between the theoretical and the practical. In more prosaic terms, the dispatcher is the one who needs to find that 0.2 of a guard.

The dispatcher needs to be intimately familiar with the post being staffed and its requirements. For example, where there are multiple posts, can the guards from one be used to cover the others? If there is going to be a vacancy, which post can be left uncovered temporarily? Are there any special training requirements? Is the post unsuitable for certain types of officers?

The dispatcher also needs an intimate knowledge of the guards he or she will be scheduling. For example, some guards deal well with the public, while others are best used in remote sites. Some officers lack the discipline or quick reactions needed to monitor physical security systems. Some guards may have physical limitations that restrict them to desk duties. It is the scheduler's job to match the appropriate guard to each post. This is the reason that the dispatcher is part of the hiring process in many companies. At a minimum, the dispatcher should meet each new guard that he or she will be dispatching.

The dispatcher has the often thankless job of making sure all posts are covered. If he or she does the job well, hardly anyone notices because the shift changes go smoothly. If the dispatcher fails, everyone from the client to the general manager will know about it. The dispatcher is the one who gets the emergency calls, the complaints, and the last minute changes and must deal with them. In some companies, the pace is so hectic that the maximum retention time of a dispatcher is two years.

The dispatcher has only two rules:

1. Thou shalt not let any post go uncovered.
2. Thou shalt not incur any unbillable overtime.

Dispatcher Tools

To meet these requirements, the dispatcher has four main tools. The first is the schedule, as prepared by the scheduler, which shows all required coverage and the scheduler's plan for meeting those requirements. Any open posts should be readily apparent.

The schedule is usually accompanied by an information sheet (Figure 6.7) that includes special instructions, client emergency information, training requirements, and so forth. The information sheet will show required coverage and may include a sample schedule showing the most cost-effective coverage. Many companies also list the names of guards who have been trained on the site and guards who, for one reason or another, are not to be used at the site.

The third tool for the dispatcher is an availability sheet that shows each guard's schedule and shows who may be available for assignment (Figure 6.8). This listing provides the dispatcher with a ready resource for various options in filling open posts.

POST INFORMATION

CLIENT:_____

CLIENT CONTACT:_____

TELEPHONE:_____

BILLING ADDRESS:

_____

_____

_____

TELEPHONE

GUARD POST:_____

EMERGENCY CONTACTS:

_____

_____

_____

_____

_____

SITE LOCATION: _____

CROSS STREET: _____

GENERAL DESCRIPTION OF DUTIES:_____

_____

_____

REQUIRED TRAINING:_____

_____

_____

SCOPE OF WORK

SHIFT	S	M	T	W	T	F	S
TOTAL							

SCHEDULE

SHIFT	S	M	T	W	T	F	S
TOTAL							

Figure 6.7 Post information sheet.

GUARD	SUN	MON	TUE	WED	THU	FRI	SAT	TOTAL HOURS

Figure 6.8 Availability sheet.

The fourth tool is a contact list—a telephone directory of home telephone numbers for all the guards, supervisors, and managers in the company.

There are several forms that are useful in managing the dispatch operation. The first is a telephone log on which the dispatcher enters all calls received during his or her shift. This is a valuable management tool that should be reviewed by the dispatcher's supervisor daily. For example, clients frequently call after hours with schedule changes or complaints. The dispatcher telephone log can record and transmit this information to management.

If the dispatcher does not also maintain payroll data, there must be a mechanism for providing shift change information to the payroll department. Many companies use a special change document to record unplanned absences, tardiness, or overtime. Others require that each dispatcher keep a daily log of all activities, messages, and changes. If the dispatcher is responsible for disciplinary actions, appropriate forms should be provided. Finally, copies of all post orders are essential reference documents for the dispatcher.

Ensuring Post Coverage

One of the main jobs of the dispatcher is to ensure post coverage. When a guard becomes ill and cannot report to his or her assigned post, the dispatcher must find a replacement as soon as possible. If it is close to the post start time (and it almost always is!), the dispatcher must react immediately. Several options are open to the dispatcher:

1. replace the guard with a part-time guard;
2. replace the guard with a full-time guard who has not been scheduled for a full forty hours;
3. replace the missing guard with a full-time guard and replace that guard on a later shift so that he or she works only forty hours;
4. hold the outgoing guard on post, find a part-timer to work four hours and accept four hours of unbillable overtime;
5. split the shift between the outgoing guard and the guard on the next shift and accept eight hours of unbillable overtime;
6. replace the guard with an off-duty full-time guard and accept eight hours of unbillable overtime;
7. get a supervisor or manager to cover the post until a replacement can be found; or
8. let the post go uncovered and find a new line of work.

There are other options, but these seem to be routinely used throughout the industry. Dispatchers have also been known to rotate officers going off shift through several posts to maintain coverage and to call in a replacement dispatcher or supervisor and cover the post themselves. They are masters at cajoling, promising, threatening, and sweet-talking reluctant guards into taking a post. It takes a special kind of person to be able to call a guard at three in the morning and persuade him or her to relieve a sick guard.

Dispatcher Standard Operating Procedures

Because dispatchers tend to be creative, management must establish clear guidelines for what is acceptable performance. Dispatchers faced with an open post are frequently willing to fill a vacancy with any available guard. They may ignore training requirements or send unsuitable guards. It is important, therefore, that the dispatcher be provided with clear, written instructions.

The dispatcher information manual or Standard Operating Procedures (SOP) should contain the following information:

1. The authority range of the dispatcher. For example, can he or she terminate guards (the dispatcher should not) or can he or she replace guards who are incapacitated, intoxicated, etc. (absolutely)? What is his or her relationship to site supervisors or mobile patrol supervisors?
2. Duties that must be performed, such as filling open posts, contacting clients, etc.
3. Standards of conduct.
4. Guidelines on contacting management, clients, outside agencies (e.g., police, fire). When should they be contacted and in what order?
5. Guidelines on filling open shifts, as discussed earlier.
6. Procedures for completing any operational forms used, such as accident reports, schedules, and account information sheets.
7. Guidelines for handling requests for service.
8. Guidelines for dealing with emergencies on posts.
9. Instructions for continuing operations during emergencies, such as earthquakes, snowstorms, etc.

Two common additional duties for dispatchers are providing guards with copies of their schedules, and confirming that guards will work as scheduled. For the most part, this is routine. Nevertheless, the company should have a formal mechanism for issuing and confirming schedules.

The size of the company will determine the feasibility of the various options open to the dispatcher. Some companies require all guards to call in on a certain day to confirm schedules. Any that do not are called by the dispatcher and appropriate disciplinary measures are taken. Some dispatchers call every guard themselves. Other companies mail a written copy of the schedule to the guard's home, often accompanying the guard's paycheck. Another effective way is to work through the lead guard or site supervisor and have them report back to the dispatcher. There is no right way. The important thing is that the guard must be notified regarding his or her schedule.

Computerized Scheduling and Dispatching

The preceding discussions have focused on the manual methods for scheduling and dispatching. While they have worked for many companies of varying sizes, they have also burned out a lot of dispatchers and entry-level managers. Thankfully, the advent of computerized scheduling has helped to change this somewhat.

It is important to realize that the computer will not do anything that could not be done manually by the scheduler/dispatcher—it merely does it faster. With a computer scheduling program, the user enters the post requirements and the list of available guards, and the program matches these up and prints out a schedule. This schedule is useless unless the scheduler has accurately entered the basic information and is willing to carefully review the schedule.

This caveat aside, a computerized scheduling program can save untold hours. Most post assignments are routine, and in the manual system, this means copying them over each week by hand. The computer allows this to be done almost instantly, requiring that the scheduler/dispatcher enter only changes to the master schedule. The program allows the entry of holidays and vacations, reminding the dispatcher when guards will be unavailable. If the dispatcher desires, the computer will fill these openings from the list of available guards. The computer can also flag guards who are not to be used on certain posts and recognize those who have had special training on the posts.

The computerized scheduling programs available today are full management tools. They can be used to record personnel data such as address, telephone number, social security number, driver's license, training records, etc. There are payroll programs that will interface directly with the data in the scheduling program. If used properly, these programs can provide a significant savings in office overhead.

From the dispatcher's perspective, the scheduling program is a godsend. The computer generates schedules without the need for rewriting post schedules that have not changed. The computer will print both a post schedule and a list, in alphabetical order, of all guards and their assignments. It will, depending on the program, print individual schedules for each guard. The touch of a few keys can provide a listing of all off-duty guards and their telephone numbers. It can then qualify that list as to who is trained and not restricted from the post, cutting decision-making time considerably. Client information sheets are also part of most programs, allowing this information to be readily accessible and to include special instructions and emergency information.

A significant advantage of computerized scheduling systems is their ability to interface with financial modules that generate payroll and billing. By updating the projected schedule to reflect actual service, the dispatcher is in effect preparing all the information needed to generate the guard's paycheck and the client's invoice. A fully integrated system can also automatically generate management reports such as a profitability report or job variation analysis.

Post Orders

An important function of the operations staff is to work with the client to determine just what is expected of the guard at each post and to translate the client's desires into written instructions for the guard. The busier the guard can be kept, the better for all concerned. Too often, a client sees the guard "doing nothing" and remembers the large bill that comes in regularly. By providing tasks for the guard, the client sees an active, alert employee who is making material contributions to the client's operations. The guard will have a more rewarding job and will remain motivated.

Each post, regardless of size, requires its own set of post instructions. The guard must clearly understand what is required at the post. Unfortunately, many companies either start up a contract without preparing post orders or allow the lead guard to develop them alone. The correct approach, whenever possible, is to meet with the client, draft post orders, provide a copy for the client's review, and use the orders to train the guards. The orders should be reviewed after the first month of operation and fine-tuned. They should be reviewed annually thereafter.

There are two schools of thought on post orders. One approach is to take a three-ring binder and fill it with all the information that the guard will ever need. The second is to provide a simple checklist on a single sheet of paper or pocket-sized card.

Post Manuals

There is a lot to be said for gathering all available information about a post into a single source. It is an excellent training tool, and an office copy can be a useful reference for the dispatcher. It can contain the instructions for on-site equipment or controls, such as the fire alarm consoles and elevator controls found in high-rise office buildings. It can record procedures not normally performed by the guards, such as emergency shutdown procedures for machinery. If a standardized format is used, similar post orders can be developed for each post and can even serve as a public relations/marketing tool. One national guard company provides to its branch offices a three-ring binder with the company logo and preprinted dividers. Several sections are already filled in with company policies and procedures. The local office types the post-specific information on matching paper stock, and the client is presented with a truly impressive set of post orders.

The problem with such orders is that they are generally read the first time a guard reports for duty and seldom thereafter. They are useful for reference but have little bearing on the guard's day-to-day job. If not reviewed, they tend to collect all manner of handwritten notes, outdated memoranda, and unnecessary information. For this reason, many companies have moved away from the manual format and are using short checklists that can be carried by the guard while on duty.

Post Order Checklists

Checklists are brief summaries of the required duties that the guard must perform on a day-to-day basis. They are designed to remind the guard of tasks to be performed through memory aids. By their very nature, they do not contain a lot of information and presuppose that the guard has been trained in how to accomplish the assigned tasks. They can be carried around by the guard during the performance of his or her duties and are more likely to be used than the guard post manual.

The drawback to checklists is that they are brief and assume adequate training. While they can be used for training, the guard has no backup reference if he or she does not remember how to perform a task. In addition, checklists generally do not contain information on tasks that are not performed routinely.

A combination of the two systems provides the optimum arrangement for communicating post orders. The standard post manual is prepared and used for training and reference. The guard also carries a checklist for routine operations. In the event of an emergency, the guard manual should contain a checklist in the appropriate section that can be pulled out and used by the guard. The use of pull-out checklists is an accepted practice in the emergency management community and works well.

Preparing Post Orders

In preparing post orders, simplicity and accuracy are paramount. If the company already has (as it should) an employee manual that has been issued to each guard (see chapter 2), there is no need to repeat company policy statements. The orders should deal with site-specific information only. If a manual is used, it must be indexed in a logical manner that makes the information easy to find, particularly when there is an emergency situation.

Post orders should be written in a style that is brief, clear, and easy to read. Reading comprehension is closely associated with the time required to read a passage. The shorter the section of information, the more easily it will be understood. The orders should be in plain text, eliminating any ambiguity and potential misunderstandings, and be precise in the choice of words. Finally, the manual should be written at a low literacy level. Many guards lack the reading skills of managerial personnel. Some use English as a second language. Consequently, manuals should be written to a level equivalent to the daily newspaper. There are several computer programs that will evaluate the reading level of a specific document.

Special Instructions

A guard's performance on post is directed by three components. The first is the company handbook carried by each guard. These are company policies and procedures applicable to all guards on all posts. Many companies refer to them as general orders. The second component is the set of instructions specific to each post, encapsulated in the post orders in whatever form is used. These instructions change only a little over time and reflect the day-to-day and emergency policies and procedures unique to a post. But what about temporary changes, one-time events, and unforeseen taskings? These form the third component of the post instructions, usually referred to as "special instructions" or "special orders."

No matter how carefully written, post orders cannot foresee every possible occurrence at a post. Nor should they try to. Instead, there must be a mechanism for communicating information to the guard that either is temporary in nature or anticipates a revision to the post orders, i.e., temporarily supersedes the post orders while a new version is being written. Examples of this are special deliveries or visits by VIPs. The best and surest way to communicate this information is in writing. A short memorandum or special checklist provided to the guard can be temporarily posted for reference on site. It can also be passed on to multiple shifts. Because the instructions are written, there is little chance of misunderstanding. Once the need for the special order is gone, it can be discarded or filed, as appropriate.

There are occasions when a written memorandum is not possible because of time constraints. To solve this problem, many companies use a "pass-down" book at each post. This is a bound ledger in which the guard writes down any special instructions that he or she has received. The book is required reading whenever a guard comes on shift. Again, because the information is written down, there is less chance that it will not be passed on to the appropriate shift for action. The problem with the pass-down book is that it is possible for the guard to misunderstand the instructions and write them down incorrectly. An incoming guard may not understand what is written. Finally, if the information is provided too far in advance, it may be buried under more recent instructions. Nevertheless, the pass-down book can work well and is much preferable to a verbal message.

Advanced Micro Devices, Inc., of California uses a creative solution to advise its large security force of changes. The company publishes a weekly newsletter that highlights procedural changes, temporary posts, and special events. The publication also identifies noteworthy achievements and promotions and serves the additional role of building team spirit among the staff.

Reports

Post orders communicate the client's desires to the guard. In the same manner, the guard must in turn communicate with the client regarding problems at the post. There are a number of ways this can be accomplished.

Post Logbook

Many companies make use of a post log. This is a bound ledger in which the guard records any incidents required by his or her instructions to be logged or that he or she feels are significant and important. Examples include the following:

- time reported for duty
- tours completed
- special reports written
- special instructions received and entered in pass-down book
- deliveries
- inspections by supervisors
- time relieved

To be effective, the post log must be checked regularly. Many companies require supervisors to read and initial the log book anytime they visit a post. Many clients do the same. The problem, however, is that the information stays with the post. It is not passed to the guard company office or to the client who does not choose to stop by and read it on a regular basis. Therefore, information may not reach the client or the guard company in a timely manner. Further, researching a problem or complaint will require a visit to the post or the removal and replacement of the post logbook.

Daily Activity Reports

Many companies use a daily activity report (DAR) rather than a logbook. The individual report records the same information as the logbook and is turned in by the guard at the end of his or her shift to an appropriate authority. Some companies require that the guard submit the report to the client; others have it sent to the company office. Still others use a multipart form with a copy for the client, office, and guard.

The individual report provides a steady flow of information from the guard on a daily basis. This information can become overwhelming and trivial. This is particularly true if the guard has not been properly trained and the report includes only hourly entries that state "3:00 Made rounds—all secure." If the individual report is used and forwarded to the client, the guard must receive clear guidance on what to report. In designing a report form, consider that the person reviewing the form may have problems reading the handwriting of the guard and the guard may not have the ability to compose lengthy narrative reports.

To avoid some of these problems, many companies have adopted the concept of exception reporting. Under this concept, the guard report focuses only on unusual occurrences or problems. The client is generally uninterested in anything other than this and appreciates not having to wade through routine reports. This type of DAR is usually a combination of a checklist that indicates the problem coupled with a narrative portion that briefly explains the problem and what corrective action was taken (see Figure 6.9). In an effort to cut down the amount of paperwork involved in DARs, several companies have developed a single report form that can be used for all three shifts. These DARs incorporate a checklist format for each shift and a narrative section for explanations of any problems noted in the checklists. This allows the reviewer to immediately note any significant events that have occurred within the previous twenty-four hours.

The appropriate mechanism for reporting will depend on the company and client involved. In general, the most effective method is exception reporting, backed up by a post log as a permanent record of routine events. This backup is essential because, while the time of a tour, for example, may not seem important on a daily basis, it may become critical during a criminal investigation or civil trial.

Incident Reports

Occasionally, an event will occur on a post that warrants a more complete explanation than that required on the DAR. For this reason, most companies use a special incident report. This report constitutes a preliminary investigation into a serious event, such as a theft or accident, and should be treated accordingly. Formats range from simple narratives (Figure 6.10) to complex checklist, block, and narrative types reminiscent of police reports (Figure 6.11). An incident report should always receive special handling and should be immediately reviewed for completeness by a member of

SECURITY DEPARTMENT
OFFICERS DAILY REPORT

REPORT OF		SHIELD NO.	SHIFT FROM	AM PM	TO	AM PM	S M T W T F S	DATE	

RELIEVED OFFICER		AM PM	RELIEVED BY OFFICER		AT	AM PM	NO. OF RADIO AND OR BEEPER ISSUED	TOTAL HRS.
	AT							

ITEMS NO. 1 THROUGH NO. 13 MUST BE CHECKED (✓) YES OR NO. ITEMS CHECKED YES MUST BE EXPLAINED UNDER "DETAILS".

DETAILS
REPORT BELOW THE DETAILS OF EACH ITEM CHECKED YES AND ALL OTHER UNUSUAL OCCURRENCES OR MATTERS OF INTEREST. LIST LICENSE NUMBERS OF ALL PARKING VIOLATORS.

	WERE THERE ANY	YES	NO	DETAILS
1	FIRE HAZARDS			
2	SMOKING VIOLATIONS			
3	DOORS OR WINDOWS OPEN OR BROKEN			
4	VAULTS OR SAFES OPEN			
5	TRESPASSER			
6	SUSPICIOUS ACTIVITIES			
7	THEFTS - ATTEMPTED			
8	THEFTS - COMMITTED			
9	PROPERTY DAMAGE			
10	SECURITY LIGHTS OFF			
11	PARKING VIOLATIONS			
12	EXITS BLOCKED			
13	SAFETY HAZARDS			

EXAMINED BY				OPERATION INSPECTED BY	
INITIALS	SGT.	LT.	CAPT.	SEC. OFF.	SIGNED
DATE					OFFICER SIGNATURE

Figure 6.9 Single-shift report. [From Guy et al., *Forms for Safety and Security Management.* (Boston: Butterworth Publishers, 1981.)]

CONTROL # _____

DATE:_____ DAY_____

TIME: _____ AM _____
PM

TYPE OF REPORT
☐ INCIDENT
☐ INVESTIGATION
☐ INFORMATION

SECURITY REPORT

PREPARED BY: _____

CATEGORY: _____ SUBJECT: _____

DETAILS _____

PAGE _____ OF _____   SIGNATURE _____

Figure 6.10 Narrative report. [From Guy et al., *Forms for Safety and Security Management.* (Boston: Butterworth Publishers, 1981.)]

SECURITY DEPARTMENT INCIDENT REPORT

OFFENSE CATEGORY		DATE-TIME RECEIVED	DAY OF WK.	DATE			TIME		INVESTIGATION NO.
				MO.	DAY	YR.		AM. PM.	
FORCED ENTRY		COMPLAINANTS NAME							HOME PHONE
THEFT	PERS. PROP.								
	COMPANY PROP.	ADDRESS							BUSINESS PHONE
	COIN MACHINE								
	AUTO	STATUS							
ROBBERY		☐ VISITOR ☐ EMPLOYEE ☐ OTHER (SPECIFY)							
ASSAULT		DATE-TIME OF OFFENSE		DAY OF WK.	DATE		TIME		
RAPE					MO. DAY YR.		AM. PM.		
MANSLAUGHTER		PLACE				WEAPON USED			
DISTURBANCE									
VANDALISM									
TRAFFIC		TRADEMARK							
OTHER (SPECIFY)									

VICTIMS NAME	ADDRESS

SEX AGE RACE	STATUS	
☐ M ☐ F		☐ VISITOR ☐ EMPLOYEE ☐ OTHER (SPECIFY)
MEDICAL TREATMENT ☐ YES (EXPLAIN) ☐ NO	DESCRIPTION OF LOST PROPERTY	VALUE

DESCRIPTION OF OFFENDER(S)

	SEX	RACE	HEIGHT	BUILD	EYES	HAIR	GLASSES	COMPLEXION
NO. 1	☐ M ☐ F						☐ YES ☐ NO	
	MARKS				AGE	HAT	COAT	SHIRT
NO. 2	SEX ☐ M ☐ F	RACE	HEIGHT	BUILD	EYES	HAIR	GLASSES ☐ YES ☐ NO	COMPLEXION
	MARKS				AGE	HAT	COAT	SHIRT

WITNESS NAME 1.	ADDRESS	TELEPHONE
WITNESS NAME 2.	ADDRESS	TELEPHONE

LAW ENFORCEMENT AGENCY NOTIFIED	TIME	PERSON
1.	A.M. P.M.	
2.	A.M. P.M.	

NAME OF PERSON ARRESTED 1.	ADDRESS
NAME OF PERSON ARRESTED 2.	ADDRESS

CHARGES

1.   2.

WAS PHYSICAL FORCE USED   ☐YES   ☐NO

SIGNATURE OF REPORTING OFFICER DATE	FOR SECURITY OFFICE USE ONLY
	APPROVED _____
	DATE NAME CARD COMPLETED _____

Figure 6.11 Block and narrative report. [From Guy et al., *Forms for Safety and Security Management.* (Boston: Butterworth Publishers, 1981.)]

management. Several companies even require that the report be completed by a supervisor rather than the guard. A good incident report should prompt the guard for the information required, as well as provide a place for a narrative and supervisor follow-up action.

Guard Tours

Developing Tours

Guard posts are generally divided into two types: stationary and roving. Stationary posts perform specific tasks, such as access control and alarm monitoring. Roving guards also may perform specific tasks, but their charter is much broader: they patrol the client's site watching for anything unusual. In most cases, the roving patrol is the best and most cost-effective use of the guard. The ability to move freely and unpredictably through a site makes the patrol guard a tremendous deterrent to crime.

The guard patrol, however, cannot be completely unstructured. The guard rapidly becomes bored, and there is no guarantee that he or she is checking all required areas. To preclude this, a guard tour should be designed with checkpoints that the guard is required to visit with a certain frequency.

Tours can be laid out any number of ways. The three basic patterns are circular, double-back, and random. In the circular pattern, the guard visits each checkpoint in order. This makes the patrol highly predictable, even when the start time is varied. The double-back pattern requires the guard to occasionally retrace his or her steps and revisit a point that has already been checked. The random pattern allows the guard to visit the checkpoints in any order, any number of times, at the time of his or her choosing. It is designed to be completely unpredictable and is the most favored patrol pattern for this reason.

Whichever pattern is used, the instructions provided to the guard must be clear. This is particularly important in the case of the random pattern. The guard must be given a minimum number of times to visit each checkpoint and a maximum time between visits. For example, the post orders might read: "Each point is to be checked a minimum of twelve times during the shift, with no more than an hour between each visit." This is to prevent the guard from not checking an area for long periods of time.

Checkpoints should always be selected with a particular purpose in mind, and the guard should clearly understand that purpose. Otherwise, the patrol becomes routine, the guard develops tunnel vision, and there is a tendency to skip checkpoints. Ideally, there should be a task to accomplish at each one, such as checking a door or window or piece of equipment. Sometimes, checkpoints are positioned to require the guard to walk through and check a large open area. He or she must know this.

Tour Management

There are many ways to ensure that a guard visits all checkpoints at the proper time interval. The simplest is a log at each checkpoint that the guard is required to sign. There is no guarantee that the guard will not remove the sign-in sheets on the first tour and replace them on the last or that the guard is not making false entries unless there are periodic inspections by a supervisor. It is extremely difficult for a supervisor to check that the guard is making all required rounds without gathering up all the sheets and checking them against the daily activity report.

The tour clock has been in use in the security industry for generations. The most common type places a key at each checkpoint. The guard carries a clock containing a paper disk. When the guard inserts the key, the post number, time, and date are recorded on the disk. The disk can then be checked by the client or a supervisor.

In actual practice, the system does not always work well. The clocks tend to be heavy and cumbersome and are not popular with guards. Although well made, they can be damaged by a disgruntled guard. The paper disk is difficult to read and frequently not checked. Even when they are checked, it is sometimes days or weeks after the tour. Unscrupulous guards have come up with several ingenious ways of compromising the system as well.

The next generation of tour-management devices—computer-based devices that use either an optical or magnetic reader—has already begun replacing the guard clock. The keys used by the clock system are replaced with vandal-proof bar codes or magnetic strips. The guard carries a reader, some as small as a credit card or pen, that scans the strip and records the location, date, and time. The guard also has the ability to scan in information from a code sheet (see Figure 6.12) that provides information concerning the checkpoint. At the end of the tour, the information contained in the reader is transferred via modem to a computer in the company's office and can then be used to produce a number of reports, allowing management to track incidents, guard performance, and recurring problems. Because all the information needed by the company and the client can be recorded using this system, daily activity reports can be virtually eliminated.

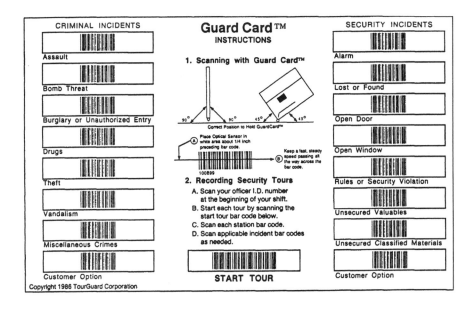

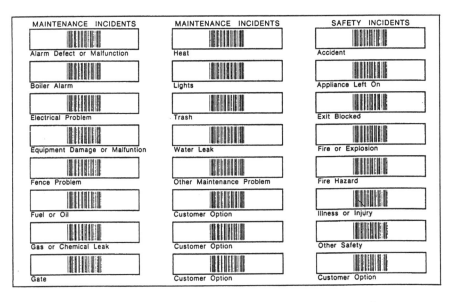

Figure 6.12 Tour code table. (Courtesy TimeKeeping Systems, Inc.)

7

Accounting

The accounting function in a guard company generally receives little emphasis aside from the tasks of billing and payroll. Yet good accounting practices and conventions can have a direct effect on profitability. Accountants try to determine precise costs and income resulting from service. By understanding the relationship between income and cost, the guard force manager can reduce expenses while remaining competitive and will be in a position to determine the profitability of a specific contract.

Accounting provides the financial management tools necessary to analyze the company's fiscal performance. It allows the careful crafting of contract rates that balance competitiveness with cost savings. It highlights problem areas such as excessive overtime or noncompliance with contractual obligations. It identifies costs that are either excessive or too low for adequate service. In many ways, accounting reports are the most vital tools available to the guard force manager.

Determining Guard Rates

Components of the Guard Rate

Many guard companies in business today do not understand the mechanism for determining the rates for guard service. Instead of using precise accounting techniques, they rely on formulas that have not been verified in some time and may not be accurate. In the highly competitive guard business, it is critical that rates be set to cover all incurred costs plus a reasonable profit yet still be kept as low as possible to remain competitive. This means that every component of the rate must be carefully calculated for each contract. In addition, many clients, particularly those with large accounts, have become quite sophisticated in understanding and comparing contract bids.

A common approach for many new companies is to use a formula to determine personnel and management costs, then add a dollar amount (or some other set amount) to cover profit. Figure 7.1 is an example of such a computation as used by one national company, resulting in this case in a rate of $6.42 per hour. Note that the company has chosen to add a factor to compensate for unbillable overtime, adding to the overall rate. Such a practice could mean the difference between winning or losing a contract. The company has also chosen to reflect a sales commission separate from the management fee. This is also a debatable policy. Sales commissions are generally charged as part of the overhead, which in this case is reflected as a management fee. If the management fee factor is accurate and does not include sales costs, then there is no problem with this method. However, if the management fee is merely a guess, adding the sales commission may again boost the rate past a competitive level.

A more sophisticated approach is to develop the rate by carefully evaluating its four basic components: direct payroll, payroll costs, overhead, and profit. Understanding these components and how they can be minimized allows the guard company manager to determine the lowest acceptable bid that can be proposed to a client. Since the difference between the winning bid and the nearest competitor's bid may be only a few pennies per hour, it is critical that the bid be as low as possible while still covering all costs and generating a reasonable profit.

Base Wage	$4.25
Overtime (4%)	.17
Payroll Taxes (17%)	.72
Uniform Costs (1%)	.05
Vacation Pay (1%)	.05
Sales Commission (2%)	.09
Management Fee (2%)	.09
Margin	1.00
Hourly Rate	6.42

Figure 7.1 Rate computation (common method).

Direct Payroll

Basic Wage

Direct payroll is the salary of the guard that performs the work. While the client may be given the option of setting salary, it is important to establish minimums based on comparable salaries for other companies. This helps to ensure that the company can attract suitable candidates for the contract. Using the minimum rate established by state and federal laws tends to reduce the number of qualified guard candidates who will apply for positions. Traditionally, companies who pay minimum wage or slightly above develop a reputation as low-end companies and seldom win bids on premium contracts because of the type of guards they recruit.

Determining the rate of pay is extremely important as there is a direct correlation between rate of pay and quality of employee. The guard force manager should have access to recent salary surveys conducted in his or her area of operation or, if a new company, should consider conducting such a survey. The U.S. Department of Labor's Bureau of Labor Statistics publishes *Area Wage Surveys* for most major metropolitan areas. These surveys address all occupations and provide only a brief treatment of guard wages. More industry-specific data can be found in the *Security Letter Source Book* published by Butterworth-Heinemann and in *Compensation in the Security/Loss Prevention Field* published by Abbott, Langer & Associates. These surveys can be used to establish a base wage scaled to the market segment that the guard company has targeted (see chapter 4). The base wage is the lowest amount the company can agree to pay its guards and still provide the level of service it promises.

Sophisticated clients will often set the base wage as part of a request for proposal (RFP) in order to facilitate the comparison of competing bids. If the client has not done so, it is in the best interest of the guard company to encourage the setting of a base wage for the contract. This allows fair competition and prevents deliberate underbidding by unscrupulous companies.

Most companies commonly pay the guard the same base wage regardless of where he or she is assigned. If the guard is experienced and has been with the company a number of years, the base wage may exceed the wage billed to the client as part of the contract rate, resulting in a loss to the guard company. If the guard is a new employee, his or her rate may be less than that being billed to the client, and the client is effectively overcharged. Either case is unacceptable. Consequently, the base wage of the guard should be determined by his or her assignment and longevity should be rewarded by pay increases negotiated as part of the contract or by transfer to a more lucrative post.

Holiday and Premium Pay

Guards are generally expected to work twenty-four hours a day, seven days a week. There are usually no shift differentials for evening or weekend work. It is an accepted practice, however, to pay guards an additional amount for working on certain holidays. These holidays are specified in the service contract and are normally paid only to guards who actually work on the holiday.

The guard company has the option of billing the client directly for each holiday or building the holiday pay into the billing rate as an hourly cost. The advantage to the latter is that the client pays one constant rate instead of a rate that varies periodically. Regardless of the method used, the specific holidays for which the guard will be paid should be clearly defined in the service contract.

Billing for holiday pay is computed by dividing the annual holiday pay by the total number of hours worked to determine the hourly cost. This hourly cost becomes part of the hourly rate. Figure 7.2 gives an example of this type of calculation. It assumes that the holiday pay is one and a half times the base wage and that the guard is paid for ten holidays. Note that all payroll costs are part of the calculation but that overhead and profit are not as they are part of the final rate.

Premium pay is usually a small amount added to a guard's salary for special or additional work. An example would be an additional amount paid to a lead guard on the day shift who serves as site supervisor. This pay is usually paid as part of the guard's base wage. However, it may be shown as a separate item if it is post-specific and/or requested by the client.

Payroll Costs

In addition to the direct salary paid to the guard, there are a number of taxes and insurance costs associated with payroll that must be calculated. Each of these payroll costs must be paid out of gross earnings and represent an expense that can be identified and covered in the billing rate.

---

10 Holidays x 8 Hours per Holiday = 80 Hours Annual Holiday

80 Hours x $7.86 [1.5 x (Base Rate of $6.42 less $1.18 profit and overhead)] = $628.80

$628.80 ÷ 2080 (Total Annual hours) = $.30 Hourly Holiday Cost

---

Figure 7.2 Holiday-pay cost computation.

Fortunately, these costs are based on a percentage of payroll and can be reduced to simple mathematical factors. These costs include the following.

Workers' Compensation Insurance

This insurance provides compensation to the employee for any job-related injury or illness. Premiums for this program are paid by the guard company to either a state-administered program or to private insurance carrier, depending on state law. Cost savings can be obtained under most programs by maintaining a low accident/illness rate. In addition, different rates are charged for different categories of employee. As with general liability insurance (chapter 3), it is to the company's advantage to distinguish between guards and clerical staff rather than lumping all employees together. Rates are calculated on the basis of $100 of payroll, allowing a rate factor to be determined by the formula $R/100$, where R is the rate. For example, a rate of $8.25 per $100 of payroll is $8.25/100 = .0825$.

State Unemployment Insurance

This program is designed to provide temporary financial assistance to a worker while he or she seeks a new job. This program is funded by employers at no cost to the employee and is charged at a rate determined by state law. This rate is based on $100 of payroll up to a maximum payroll base. Federal standards are 5.4 percent on a base of $7,000, but actual cost varies from state to state. Because of the high turnover in the guard industry, it is difficult to realize any savings on unemployment insurance costs. However, since it is possible to deny benefits based on voluntary discharge or termination for cause, a good terminations program can have an impact on these costs (see chapter 5).

Federal Unemployment Insurance (FUI)

Unemployment programs are administered by the state but carried out under federal supervision under the Federal Unemployment Tax Act, which is part of the Internal Revenue Service Code. Funds collected under this act are used to supplement state programs in times of high unemployment or when the benefit period is extended by special legislation, as it was in the mid-1980s. The act requires a payment of 6.2 percent on the first $7,000 of wages paid to an employee but credits the employer with taxes paid into state programs, up to 5.4 percent. Since all states adhere to the qualifying guidelines contained in the Act, the effective rate for FUI is 0.8 percent.

Basic Wage		4.25
Workers' Comp	(.0825)	.350
SUI	(.0540)	.230
FUI	(.0080)	.034
FICA	(.0715)	.303
General Liability	(.0380)	.161
Hourly Cost	(.2540)	1.078 = $1.08 Hourly Cost

Figure 7.3 Payroll cost computation.

Federal Insurance Contributions Act

This contribution matches the contribution of the employee paid into the Social Security system. The amount is specified by law and increases over time. Currently, it is 7.15 percent.

General Liability Insurance

As was discussed in chapter 3, liability insurance is based on salary and category of personnel. This rate can be factored into the guard rate.

Once the percentage factors for each of these payroll costs are known, it is possible to calculate the total payroll costs for a specific salary level. Figure 7.3 shows such a calculation based on the federal minimum wage level of $4.25.

Variable Overhead Costs

Overhead costs are costs associated with the running of a business. They can be costs that are fixed, such as rent and management salaries, or they may vary based on the amount of business done. Such costs can be directly billed to the client in some cases or may need to be indirectly billed by calculating them as part of the hourly billing rate.

Direct payroll costs are based on percentages of the actual salary of the guard. Variable costs, on the other hand, will change depending on a number of factors, such as longevity, contract requirements, and so forth. These costs include the following.

Vacation Pay

Vacation pay is an incentive for an employee to remain on the job. It is viewed as a reward for faithful service and a period for rest and relaxation. It is not uncommon in the guard business, however, for an employee to accept a cash payment in lieu of actual time off.

Recent court decisions have held that vacation pay is a component of the employee's salary and must be paid on a prorated basis if the employee is terminated. Consequently, vacation pay can be considered a variable cost and calculated into the billing rate as part of overhead. For example, an employee who is in a category earning two weeks' vacation pay earns eighty hours pay at the base wage. This amount is divided by the number of hours worked in a year to give an hourly cost that can be added into the billing rate. Figure 7.4 shows an example of such a calculation. Note that all payroll costs are computed and added in as well.

Vacation pay is normally paid at the guard's wage at the time vacation is due. It is therefore necessary to calculate vacation pay by projecting the guard's base wage after one year rather than using the initial starting wage.

Sick Leave

Normally, guard companies do not provide sick leave as part of a benefits package. When the contract calls for this benefit, the hourly cost of such leave must be calculated as part of the billing rate. This cost is calculated by multiplying the number of allowable sick leave hours by the base wage and payroll cost factor and dividing by the number of hours worked in the year.

Medical and Life Insurance

These benefits are normally not part of the standard guard contract. To attract better-qualified candidates, the guard company may choose to offer them, or the client may request them as part of the contract. If the client does not wish to pay for benefits directly, the hourly cost can be calculated into the billing rate by dividing the annual cost by the total annual hours worked.

Other overhead costs, such as those that follow, relate directly to business rather than to personnel costs. Again, some can be billed directly to the client, but others will have to be billed indirectly through the hourly rate.

4.25 (Basic Wage) x 80 Hours (Vacation) = $340.00
1.08 (Payroll Costs) x 80 Hours (Vacations) = $ 86.40

                                                $426.40

$426.40 ÷ 2080 (Total Annual Hours) = $.21 Hourly Cost

Figure 7.4 Vacation-pay cost computation.

Uniform Costs

There are several costs associated with uniforms. These are the initial cost of the uniform, the cost of replacement components over time, and routine maintenance costs. Initial and replacement costs are usually considered part of the operating costs of the company and allocated to overhead. The exception is where a client requests a special uniform that can be used only on the client's site. The cost of a client-specific uniform can be billed directly to the client by dividing the annual cost of the uniforms by the annual number of hours worked to arrive at a component of the hourly rate. Some companies pay a small sum to the guards for maintenance of the uniforms. This component can also be calculated as part of the billing rate.

Training Costs

Training costs can be either general costs, such as preassignment training, or costs directly related to the contract. Most clients will specify site-specific training but will not pay for it directly. In this case, the cost of the training must be calculated into the billing rate. This is done by dividing the estimated annual training cost by the estimated annual hours to be worked, excluding training, to determine an hourly rate. The national average for the hiring and initial training of a security guard is approximately $600 per guard (Dalton, 1991, p. 46).

Equipment and Vehicle Costs

Any specialized equipment that will be used at the client site can be reflected in the billing rate. However, this practice distorts revenues and can lead to a false profit picture. Wherever possible, vehicles and equipment should be billed directly to the client and not be part of the hourly rate. These costs should be calculated into the rate only if the client does not wish to pay them directly.

Supervisory Costs

As the number of guards increases, there will be a corresponding increase in the amount of supervision that must be supplied by the guard company. A portion of these costs can be allocated to a client by approximating the amount of supervision needed. For example, if the company uses a rule of thumb of one dispatcher and/or field supervisor per so many guard hours, it is easy to calculate supervisory costs by multiplying the cost of a supervisor by the percentage of those hours that the contract represents. For example, if a company uses one supervisor for every 5,000 hours of weekly coverage, a client contracting for 400 hours of coverage would be billed 400/5,000 or .08 of the cost of a field supervisor.

Fixed Overhead Costs

Fixed overhead costs include all expenses of the company that do not vary or vary only slightly with increased business. Examples include management and administrative payroll, rent on office facilities, company vehicles, sales costs, utilities, and so forth. Although calculating these costs is relatively simple, most guard companies tend to guess at fixed overhead.

Overhead costs are historical costs that can be determined by examining the annual operating statement. The operating statement is a summary of expenses incurred and revenues received over the month. Certain costs, such as rent and utilities, are actual costs. Others, such as uniform purchase or automobile expenses, may be prorated as a portion of the annual budget. By dividing the expenses by the total hours billed, it is possible to calculate the cost per hour for each line item. By adding these costs per hour, it is possible to determine the overhead cost per hour of service.

Since the overhead cost is historical, it is usually based on the previous year's costs plus a factor for inflation. The guard company manager must estimate costs and revenues for the upcoming year prior to setting the overhead cost factor to be used in client billing. If the analysis is off, rates may be too low to cover overhead or too high to remain competitive. To build in a hedge, many guard companies express the overhead factor as a percentage of the hourly wage, similar to the method for figuring payroll costs. Again, this must be balanced against the need to remain competitive.

Calculating Profit

Profit is the amount of money the guard company expects to keep after it has paid the guards and covered all expenses. The actual percentage of profit expected by the company is a management decision and may vary based on the desire to win a particular contract or to compensate for a risky one. New guard companies generally make one of two mistakes: a flat dollar amount is added to the rate, or the percentage of profit is calculated using payroll, payroll cost, and overhead. To be accurate, profit must be computed on the final billing rate, not the total cost. Figure 7.5 shows the difference in these three methods of calculation. Note that while costs are the same in each calculation, the amount of profit and the billing rate vary. If the profit is calculated as a percentage of cost (as in column A of Figure 7.5), the profit is always too low. When calculated on the basis of a flat amount (as in column B of figure 7.5), it may be too high or too low.

	A	B	C
Payroll	4.25	4.25	4.25
Payroll Costs	1.08	1.08	1.08
Overhead	1.00	1.00	1.00
	6.33	6.33	6.33
Profit	.63	1.00	.70
RATE	6.95	7.33	7.03
ACTUAL PROFIT	9%	14%	10%

Desired Profit = 10%

A = Computed as 10% of $6.33 (payroll, payroll cost, overhead). Actual profit is too low. Rate could affect profitability.

B = Computed by adding $1.00 (flat dollar amount). Actual profit is too high. Rate could affect competitiveness.

C = Computed as (6.33/.9) – 6.33 (computed using the final billing rate).

Figure 7.5   Profit computation.

The formula for computing the hourly billing rate is

$$\frac{C}{1-pp}$$

where C = total cost and pp = desired rate of profit.

Column C of Figure 7.5 shows the correct computation of billing rate. In this case, total cost per hour is $6.33 and the desired rate of profit is 10%, or .10. Using the formula above,

$$\text{hourly billing rate} = \frac{\$6.33}{1-.10}$$

$$= \frac{\$6.33}{.9}$$

$$= \$7.03$$

The profit can then be computed by subtracting total costs per hour from the hourly billing rate. This effectively gives the following formula:

$$\text{profit per hour} = \frac{C}{1-pp} - C$$

Determining Contract Rates

Base Rate

The base rate is determined by adding the four basic components: payroll, payroll costs, overhead, and profit. In the simplest contract, the total contract hours are multiplied by the base rate. Most contracts, however, will use multiple rates. For each rate, determine the base wage, then compute using the fixed overhead costs and the formulas for payroll costs and profit. Determine the total contract hours for each rate and multiply by the appropriate rate. Figure 7.6 shows a simple 1-24-7 contract where the day-shift guard is paid a premium as the lead guard.

As an incentive for guards to remain with a particular site, contracts will often specify an increase in salary over time. While the client should be billed based on the salary actually paid to the guard, the contract will need to project the total annual billing and the effective hourly billing rate. Figure 7.7 shows this calculation based on stepped increases over a one-year contract. In the case where the client prefers a single rate through the life of the contract, the effective hourly billing rate can be used.

Overtime Rate

Federal and state laws dictate the payment of special overtime pay whenever a guard's working hours exceed certain maximums. This is

---

40 Hours Per Week @ $7.03 + .32 (.25 Premium + Costs) = $294.00
128 Hours Per Week @ $7.03 = $899.84

2080 Hours @ $7.35 = $15,288.00
6656 Hours @ $7.03 = $46,791.68

TOTAL WEEKLY RATE $294.00 + $899.84 = $1193.84

TOTAL ANNUAL RATE $15,288.00 + $46,791.68 = $62,079.68

Figure 7.6 Simple contract.

Payroll	4.25	4.50	4.75
Payroll Cost	1.08	1.14	1.21
Overhead	1.00	1.00	1.00
Profit	.70	.74	.77
RATE	7.03	7.38	7.73

3 Months (520 Hours)	@ 7.03 = $3655.60
3 Months (520 Hours)	@ 7.38 = $3837.60
6 Months (1040 Hours)	@ 7.73 = $8039.20

TOTAL ANNUAL BILLING	$15,532.40
Divided by Total Hours	2,080
ANNUAL EFFECTIVE RATE	$7.47

Figure 7.7 Effective annual rate computation.

usually over forty hours per week but may include hours worked over eight or ten hours in a twenty-four-hour period. In some cases, such as when overtime is a required part of a shift or covered internally as described in chapter 6, the overtime costs can be built into the rate.

Overtime rates are determined by establishing the overtime wage (usually one and a half times the base wage) and calculating the other components of the rate. This is straightforward for payroll costs. However, the guard company manager has several options to consider when determining the overhead and profit components of the rate.

The simplest method is, of course, to calculate all components of the overtime rate as one would for any other rate. However, in the case of overtime, overhead does not change as a result of the increase in rate, so the manager has the option of holding the overhead constant. It is also possible to hold profit constant, effectively charging the client only for the additional pay that will go to the guard.

For small contracts, it is a generally accepted practice to quote an overtime rate that is one and a half times the base rate. However, as the size of the contract increases, it may be advantageous to use one of the more accurate methods of overtime computation to achieve a more competitive bid. Figure 7.8 compares the four methods of computing the overtime rate.

If the company decides to build in eight hours of overtime per week rather than use a floating guard, the calculation remains fairly simple. The total number of overtime hours per year are multiplied by the overtime rate,

	Base Rate	Full Rate	O/H Constant	O/H, Profit Constant
Payroll	4.25	6.38	6.38	6.38
Payroll Cost	1.08	1.62	1.62	1.62
Overhead	1.00	1.53	1.00	1.00
Profit	.70	1.06	1.00	.70
RATE	7.03	10.59	10.00	9.70

OPTIONAL RATE: $7.03 (Base Rate) x 1.5 = $10.54

Figure 7.8   Overtime rate computation.

then divided by the total contract hours to arrive at an hourly cost. This cost can then be added into the base rate as part of the payroll component.

Contract Proposal

Simply put, the contract proposal is nothing more than the aggregation of the various hours and rates called for by the client. It is usually presented as an annual cost, broken down by various rate categories. However, a truly competitive bid is the result of careful analysis of the client's requirements balanced against the need to keep costs as low as possible.

The starting point is the development of a basic schedule, taking advantage of all the techniques available to reduce the number of required guards to the absolute minimum level. This should include the planned used of part-time guards paid at lower rates, if possible, and the limited application of built-in overtime (see chapter 6).

The second step in developing the proposal is to develop the various rates called for in the base schedule. Overtime, vacations, holidays, and benefits should all be calculated as both annual and hourly rates. If necessary, the basic schedule can be modified to allow the use of more competitive rates. Consideration should be given to the use of on-site managers and supervisors.

Once the schedule and rates have been developed, the final proposal is prepared (see chapter 4). For larger contracts, it is advantageous to break out the specifications by post rather than lumping them all together. This provides a clearer picture to the client of how the company intends to meet the contract requirements.

Payroll and Billing

The Relationship between Billing and Payroll

Every guard force manager must have an understanding of the relationship between the contract, payroll, and billing. These three factors directly affect the profitability of the company and must be accurate and precise.

The contract describes the services that the guard company has agreed to provide and the price that the client agrees to pay for those services. The guard company translates the contract requirements into a schedule of work that can be used to develop a budget for that particular contract. Guards perform services at the client site based on this schedule of work and expect to be paid. In the optimum situation, the client is billed for all work performed by the guards, and the contract is fulfilled as planned. Unfortunately, guards are occasionally sick or absent and requirements for coverage change. In such cases, the schedule of work may be very different from the actual hours worked.

The actual guard hours worked must be paid to the guard and represent an expense to the guard company. This expense must be apportioned between the client and the guard company. If the hours worked conform to the contract, all the expense is borne by the client. Additional hours, such as overtime not chargeable to the client or training time, must be absorbed by the company.

Computing Payroll

With the advent of the computer, payroll has become an extremely easy task, yet few guard companies take advantage of this technology. Most use a payroll service. Payroll companies normally require that the guard company do some preliminary payroll preparation before the service computes all required deductions and issues the actual paycheck. The preparatory work can be extensive, and many companies, including major national companies, still perform payroll calculations manually. There are a number of very viable alternatives.

One basic method of streamlining payroll is to use an *exception system*. In this system, all full-time guards are assumed to work a forty-hour week, and this is automatically calculated and paid. Adjustments for tardiness, absence, and overtime are then entered as exceptions. This reduces the amount of time needed to process payroll, as most guards will work their standard shift and only special cases must be dealt with.

A second alternative is to use computerized scheduling and payroll systems. The scheduler develops a projected schedule that is modified throughout the pay period to reflect actual hours worked. At the end of the pay period, the data is automatically transferred to a payroll program or to a payroll service.

With the advent of computerized tour-management systems, much basic information on hours worked can be downloaded by modem and then extracted through the reporting formats. This summarized information either can be used to prepare manual payrolls or can be electronically transferred to other programs.

Computing Billing

Determining how much to charge the client can be simple or complex depending on how the company has set up the billing system. If a computerized system is used, the billing is automatic. Guard hours are entered into the program and used to compute both billing and payroll. If the billing is computed manually and a bill typed, it becomes more difficult.

In simplest terms, client billing merely involves determining how many of the actual hours worked can be charged to the client. The hours are then charged to the client at the appropriate contract rate. If the contract is complex, the client must be charged the appropriate rate for the guard. For example, if a guard at the high rate of pay was replaced by a new guard at a lower rate of pay, this should be reflected in the bill, if these rates were part of the contract.

The client must also be billed for any expense incurred at the client's request. If a guard was asked to remain on post because of a special event, the client should be billed for the additional hours at the overtime rate specified in the contract.

Accuracy in billing is important to maintaining client confidence. Sophisticated clients will maintain their own records of hours worked and will compare them with the bill. If the hours billed are inaccurate, even if in the client's favor, there is an element of doubt generated as to the competency of the guard company's management.

Budgeting

Budgeting is the method used by businesses to represent future plans in financial terms. It provides a yardstick against which the company can measure progress and control costs. It can be adjusted to reflect changes in plans or can be used to determine the profitability of goods or services. It is the single most important financial management tool used by the guard company.

Budgets are divided into *capital budgets* and *operating budgets.* Capital budgets involve the acquisition of company resources with a long-term use. An example would be the purchase of a company vehicle or radio equipment. The operating budget is a short-range planning tool and covers a single year.

Operating budgets focus on revenues (i.e., how much the company expects to earn from guard contracts) and on costs. These costs may be fixed operating expenses, such as rent payments, or variable costs, such as guard salaries. They may also be semivariable and fluctuate indirectly with revenue. An example might be supervisor salaries where the addition of a certain number of contract hours requires the hiring of a new supervisor.

Costs are projected and, in some cases, prorated over the twelve-month period. This proration avoids distorting the profit picture each month with one-time expenses. For example, the printing of report forms and guard manuals in August is a one-time expense. However, this added expense would make it appear that August was a poor month in terms of profit. Consequently, the projected cost is divided over the twelve-month period to even things out.

Each month, the company should produce an operating statement that reflects actual revenues and operating costs for that month. Note that an accounting month does not necessarily equate to a calendar month. Again, this is to ensure accuracy when comparing one month to another. The monthly operating statement is then compared to the operating budget for that month. The guard manager then determines whether the variances are significant or not (Figure 7.9). An annual operating statement is used to analyze the entire year in the same manner.

Analyzing Profitability

There are a number of accounting tools available to the guard force manager to determine if the company is on track. The first is the monthly operating statement just discussed. By examining each line item as a percentage of sales (Figure 7.9), it is possible to identify areas that are absorbing more than their fair share of revenue. It is also possible to identify underfunded functions or to make decisions regarding increasing levels of funding to different functions.

The second is a weekly or biweekly analysis report or operating report. This report breaks out, by client site, the total numbers of hours worked and billed to the client and the total hours of overtime worked and either billed to the client or absorbed by the guard company. By closely examining this report, the manager can determine where problem areas are developing. Exam-

XYZ COMPANY
OPERATING STATEMENT
July 31 - September 3, 1994

	ACTUAL	% SALES	BUDGET	VARIANCE
REVENUES				
Guard Service	$75,231.00		$78,000.00	- 4%
Equipment Rental	$ 0.00		$ 0.00	
TOTAL REVENUE	$75,231.00		$78,000.00	- 4%
DIRECT PERSONNEL COSTS				
Regular Pay	$48,900.15	65.00%	$50,000.00	- 2%
Overtime/Premium Pay	$ 2,256.93	3.00%	$ 2,000.00	13%
Holiday/Vacation Pay	$ 744.79	0.99%	$ 800.00	- 7%
Payroll Costs	$ 8,726.80	11.60%	$ 8,500.00	3%
Other Benefits	$ 443.86	0.59%	$ 500.00	-11%
OTHER DIRECT EXPENSES				
Uniform Amortization	$ 925.34	1.23%	$ 1,000.00	- 7%
Liability Insurance	$ 135.42	0.18%	$ 150.00	-10%
Other Expenses	$ 270.83	0.36%	$ 300.00	-10%
GENERAL/ADMIN EXPENSES				
Regular Pay	$ 3,851.83	5.12%	$ 4,000.00	- 4%
Overtime/Premium Pay	$ 37.62	0.05%	$ 50.00	-25%
Payroll Costs	$ 489.00	0.65%	$ 500.00	- 2%
Office Rental	$ 225.89	0.30%	$ 225.00	0%
Telephone	$ 338.54	0.45%	$ 400.00	-15%
Utilities	$ 150.46	0.20%	$ 150.00	0%
Equipment Rental	$ 315.97	0.42%	$ 250.00	26%
Postage	$ 90.28	0.12%	$ 100.00	-10%
Advertising	$ 75.23	0.10%	$ 150.00	-50%
Sales Expense	$ 45.14	0.06%	$ 50.00	-10%
Printing	$ 142.94	0.19%	$ 150.00	- 5%
Other G/A Expenses	$ 150.46	0.20%	$ 300.00	-50%
TOTAL EXPENSES	$68,317.48	90.81%	$ 69,575.00	- 2%
OPERATING INCOME	$ 6,913.52	9.19%	$ 8,425.00	-18%
OTHER INCOME/EXPENSE	$ 368.63	0.49%	$ 300.00	23%
NET INCOME	$ 6,544.89	8.70%	$ 8,125.00	-19%

Figure 7.9   Operating statement.

ples of these problems are excessive unbillable overtime, uncovered posts, and excessive turnover generating increased training costs.

A third measure of profitability is a comparison between budgeted and actual hours worked. In chapter 6, there is a discussion on how to develop staffing levels for a particular post based on the following formula:

$$\text{number of guards required} = \frac{\text{total contract hours}}{\text{number of available hours}}$$

The resulting factor was used to determine the number of guards needed for a particular post. This figure also provides the number of man-year equivalents that must be budgeted for at that particular post. If the post does not run a full year, the same formula will translate the actual number of guards required into man-year equivalents. By adding man-year equivalents for all posts on a contract, it is possible to derive the number of guards that must be budgeted for in a given period and the actual number of guards needed to staff the post. Dividing the number of budgeted hours by actual hours worked using the following formula provides the actual man-year equivalent worked:

$$\frac{\text{actual man hours worked}}{\text{budgeted man hours}}$$

Comparing the actual and the budgeted man-year equivalents allows the manager to determine if the contract is over or below budget. An over-budget contract needs immediate management attention to bring it back on track. An under-budget contract may not be in full compliance with all terms of the contract and should be checked closely.

These three methods of analyzing profitability allow the manager to identify specific problem areas for correction. They do not in themselves provide a measure of overall company profitability. To do this it is necessary to collect much of the data used in the these methods and compare the results to industry norms.

Overall profitability can be measured by computing the ratios of revenues versus a particular factor. In the simplest example, the company subtracts total expenses from total revenues to determine net income. However, there are several other measures that can help the guard company manager more precisely determine where the company may be experiencing problems.

The first major measure of profitability is the *billing margin,* also known as the *gross payroll profit.* This is derived by subtracting site payroll from contract revenues. The billing margin helps the manager determine whether revenues are adequate to support the personnel costs of the service being provided. Industry averages range from 32 percent to 42 percent but may vary from this range depending on the level of off-site support needed for the contract. Significant variances in the billing margin can highlight billing problems or errors.

By subtracting all site personnel costs from contract revenue, the manager computes the *labor margin.* Like the billing margin, the labor margin is used to determine whether revenues are covering personnel costs. By comparing the labor margin to the billing margin, the manager can determine if profitability is being affected by personnel costs other than payroll.

The *direct margin* is computed by subtracting all site costs from contract revenues and is used to spot problems in supporting costs such as vehicle expenses, uniform costs, and so forth. Industry averages for direct margins range from 20 percent to 24 percent of revenues.

The next level of analysis factors is the cost of administration and is known as the *operating income*. A comparison of the operating income to the direct margin will reveal if too much overhead is being carried by the company. By comparing operating income with net income, the manager can determine if the company is excessively leveraged, is paying too much in taxes, or has other problems with expenses above those considered in the operating income.

A final measure of profitability is to compare before and after tax income with industry norms. Pretax income in well-run companies can range from 3.5 percent to 6.5 percent, with after-tax income ranging from 2.2 percent to 3.7 percent. Ideally, the company's earnings from year to year should remain relatively stable without excessive highs or lows.

Computerization

While all the analytical tools discussed in this chapter can be derived manually, it is clear that there is an overwhelming advantage to developing an integrated computer system that handles payroll and billing and automatically prints analysis reports. Such a system puts decision-making tools at the manager's fingertips in time to influence events rather than after the fact. It can reduce the number of staff required to run the guard office and make the staff more efficient.

A computerized billing system provides flexibility in serving the client by enabling the billing cycle to be more responsive to the client rather than be tied to the payroll cycle. It can also reduce the amount of time between performance of service and payment by the client, thereby increasing cash flow. American Protective Services, Inc., a California-based security company, successfully reduced this delay from sixty-two days to forty-three in less than a year (Pederson, 1993, p. 46).

8

Logistics

To properly conduct its business, a company needs to acquire certain items to help it get the job done. These range from basics, such as desks, chairs, and file cabinets, through office supplies to expensive items, such as vehicles, computers, and communications systems. These purchases represent an investment to the company and may become part of the assets reflected on the company balance sheet. They can also be a subtle drain on the profits of the company.

Like any other function of the guard company, the acquisition and accountability of property must be managed and supervised. To properly function, the guard company must have needed items on a timely basis. Because the guard company operates on a narrow profit margin, these items must be acquired in the most cost-effective manner possible.

Purchasing

As noted in chapter 7, there are certain fixed costs involved in doing business, which are largely uncontrollable. There are, however, a number of controllable *variable* costs. Nowhere is this more evident than in the purchasing of supplies and equipment. In most offices, particularly those of small companies, purchasing decisions are left to untrained employees and clerks, and no system is established to control waste and abuse. The result is that small businesses tend to pay more per item than larger companies with purchasing departments and established procedures. One expert has estimated that these overpayments equal approximately 30 percent of a small office's consumable purchases (Snodgrass, 1986, p. 21).

The main culprit is the practice of single-source purchasing. The inexperienced employee establishes a source for needed items and continues to use the same vendor for all future purchases. Orders are placed on an "as needed" basis, often with a short deadline because of immediate need. Because items are ordered as needed rather than in bulk, the order is usually too small to qualify for quantity discounts.

The first step to controlling this waste is to establish a system for purchases that involves management oversight. The most common method is a *purchase order system*. The purchase order is completed by the purchaser but must be signed by a member of management other than the purchaser. Under no circumstances should a blank purchase order be signed; all relevant cost data must be listed on the purchase order. A copy of the purchase order is filed and used to complete a receiving report when the merchandise is received and checked. The receiving report is then provided to the accounting staff where it is audited and compared with a file copy of the purchase order and a check is issued to the vendor. The purchase order system creates an audit trail that can be used to reduce the possibility of fraud and abuse.

Before an order can be placed, the purchaser must have an idea of what is needed. There are several management tools that should be used to determine those needs. The first is a *most-used-items analysis*. This analysis allows the purchaser to determine which items will represent the bulk of purchases made by the company and assists in developing a stockage level for items to be kept on hand.

Items sitting in inventory represent a cost to the company. They have been purchased with working capital and are producing no return on investment. Consequently, it is essential to avoid overordering. Inventories should be developed for the most-used items that include a minimum reorder point (i.e., when the number on hand reaches a certain number, the item is reordered) and a maximum number to be ordered when this minimum point is reached. These numbers should be in recognizable units that can be checked visually on a daily basis; they should not require a regular inventory.

One tool for tracking usage is the requisition form. While it may seem an unnecessary level of bureaucracy in a small company, it can provide data on items used, track abuse and waste, and assist in the maintenance of a master inventory. It can also be used to allocate expenses to a particular client or job site. Regardless of the system used, the company must have some method in place to track usage and control inventory. This is critical in avoiding overordering, in preventing running out of critical items unexpectedly, and in taking advantage of bulk order discounts.

Once the purchaser knows what must be ordered, he or she needs to find a source for the items. Anyone charged with the duties of purchasing must be constantly on the lookout for new sources of product. They should request catalogs, visit trade shows and vendor warehouses, and develop a resource directory. There can be no loyalty to a specific vendor unless that vendor consistently outperforms competitors.

The heart of the purchasing process is the request for quotation. This involves providing selected vendors with a list of the items that the company desires to purchase. Each vendor then submits a quotation that is analyzed by the purchaser. There are two ways to analyze the quotations: lowest overall price and lowest item price. In using the first method, the purchaser places the order with the vendor whose bottom-line price is the lowest. A disadvantage to this is that the prices on individual items may be higher than those of other vendors. In the lowest-item price method, the purchaser looks for the best price on each item and places the order with multiple vendors to assure the lowest possible price. A disadvantage of this system is that it involves tracking multiple orders instead of a single order.

Price alone is not the sole consideration for the purchaser. The quality of the product may be extremely important, particularly when ordering safety equipment. However, there are many reputable products that do not carry brand names, and the purchaser should investigate these alternatives. One way to do this is to request test samples of new products. If the potential order is large, vendors are extremely receptive to such requests.

Quality of service is another factor. A vendor who delivers late, provides incomplete or incorrect merchandise, or will not respond to complaints is probably not worth dealing with, even if his or her prices are the lowest in town.

By balancing price, quality, and service and by consistently selecting the vendor with the lowest possible prices, the company can save a tremendous amount of capital. The same technique of developing a vendor list, developing a list of needed items, requesting quotations, and selecting the qualified vendor with the lowest price can be used to purchase any item. For example, it could be used to purchase printing services, a major expense for guard companies because of the need for reports, payroll documents, manuals, and so forth. The savings of even a few cents per page for this kind of volume can be substantial.

Leasing

A company requiring a certain expensive asset has three options for obtaining that asset: renting, purchasing, or leasing. Because rental costs are extremely high, renting is usually used for short-term requirements. For example, a guard company that has a requirement for a surveillance camera for a one-time investigation may choose to rent the needed equipment. This would be preferable to buying a camera system that may be used only once. For an asset that will be needed over the longer term, leasing is the more viable option.

A lease is a contract between the owner of the asset and a second party that permits that second party to use the asset for a specified period of time in exchange for a specified payment. There are two types of leases: an *operating lease* and a *capital lease.* For accounting and tax purposes, the capital lease is treated as a loan for the purchase of the asset. This type will not be discussed here. The more common form of lease is the operating lease.

There are significant advantages to leasing that should be considered by the guard company. The first is the obvious savings in immediate outflow of working capital: there is no need for a large down payment. There are significant tax advantages, as the asset does not reflect on the company's balance sheet as would a purchase. The lease cost can be budgeted evenly over the life of the lease. An operating lease generally includes service and maintenance.

Another major advantage of a lease is that it does not saddle the company with obsolete or devalued equipment. For example, if the company buys a patrol car, it owns that car after the note is paid. The car has been taxed as an asset, has incurred maintenance expenses, and has a limited resale value. A leased patrol car, on the other hand, can be surrendered every two years and a new model leased. The same is true for copiers, computers, and fax machines, which undergo substantial product improvement over a short period of time.

The decision to lease or purchase an item is made after a lease-purchase comparison, which is an analysis of the two courses of action prepared by the accounting function. It factors in tax liabilities, costs and expenses, present and future values, and any other relevant financial data. The result of the comparison is a recommendation to management as to whether it should purchase or lease the asset.

Property Management

Accountability

Once property is acquired, the company must ensure that it is put to the use intended and not stolen or misused. This process is known as *property accountability.* It is important to realize that not all property needs to be formally accounted for. Some items, by virtue of their cost or use, do not readily lend themselves to a formal property accountability system. An example of this would be expendable items, such as batteries, that have a low cost and are used frequently. In the case of expendable items, usage tracking is sufficient to spot any abuse.

Accountability begins with the receipt of the item. The receiver must verify that the item is what is ordered and verify the invoice for payment. If the item is determined to be accountable property, the receiver must place it into the company's inventory.

There are a number of ways to maintain an inventory. Most major items have serial numbers that can be recorded in company files. Company identification tags can also be used. Tags have the advantage of clearly identifying the item as company property. If the tag incorporates a bar code, inventory management can be extremely simple. For example, a supervisor sent to inventory a client site merely enters a location code in the bar code reader, then scans all the bar codes on the company property at that site. The reader is then downloaded to a computer at the company office, and the data compared to the master inventory list. This type of system can be easily developed and used in conjunction with the guard-tour-management systems discussed in chapter 6.

Issue and Recovery of Property

Company property can be issued in two ways: as individual property or as site property. Individual property, such as uniforms and equipment, is issued to a specific individual for personal use while engaged in company business. The property must be returned upon termination of employment. Site property, such as the furniture used in the company office or at a client site, is used by multiple individuals who have a collective responsibility for the property.

Records of issued property must be carefully maintained and reviewed periodically. There must be a system in place to recover issued items in the event of a termination of an employee or a contract. Many companies place a personal-issue record in the individual guard's personnel folder so that it will be acted on when the record is processed. This system works well if the personnel record is reviewed immediately upon termination of the employee. It makes it extremely difficult, however, to perform an inventory of all property if each personnel folder must be checked. A better system is to maintain a formal property file in a central location under the supervision of a specific individual. All terminations would then need to be cleared through that individual.

Site property should be handled in a similar manner. An accurate inventory should be maintained in a central location. When a site is no longer active, all company property is recovered or accounted for using this inventory record. Bear in mind that this system can also work in reverse. Clients frequently provide equipment such as emergency keys to the guard company. This property must also be accounted for and returned to the client.

To ensure that all equipment is turned in or recovered, many companies use a *clearance sheet system*. This is a checklist that must be completed anytime an employee is terminated and is filed with the employee's personnel records. A similar checklist can be written for client sites.

Uniforms and Equipment

Uniform Styles

Since Alan Pinkerton started the first contract security force in Chicago in 1860, uniforms have played an important role in private security. The uniform is what sets the security guard apart from other employees and is a visible symbol of his or her authority. It also projects the company image, inherent in the style, color, and type of uniform selected by the company and how it is worn.

There are many different styles of uniforms in use today. However, most fall into three general categories: the traditional or police style, the corporate look, and the paramilitary or SWAT style. There is a fourth type that has been developed for use at special events—the nonuniform look. This type of "uniform" is found at events such as rock concerts, where security must be identifiable but low-key, and consists of little more than a tee-shirt, baseball cap, name tag, or other identifying item (see Figure 8.1). The nonuniform has very little place in mainstream security work and should not be an option normally available to a client.

The traditional uniform—consisting of a matching or contrasting shirt and trousers, police style jacket, and utility belt (see Figure 8.2)—evolved from attempts to have the security guard resemble a police officer. Close identification with a police uniform is thought to transfer some of the inherent authority of the police officer to the guard. It takes advantage of the psychological reaction most people have to a police uniform. Consequently, the traditional uniform is thought to be a strong deterrent to crime. By the same token, this type of uniform has a very strong image that might be inappropriate in certain settings or incompatible with a particular client's corporate image.

To soften the harshness of the police style uniform, many companies have adopted a blazer, tie, and slacks combination (see Figure 8.3). This is particularly effective with corporate clients, for whom the blazer jacket and tie can be coordinated with the corporation's colors and logo. The softer image and the presence of a tie greatly enhance the ability of the guard to deal with business professionals. On the other hand, the guard's ability to deal with the criminal element or to be readily identified in an emergency may be minimized.

Figure 8.1   Nontraditional uniform (courtesy of Commercial Detective Agency, North Arlington, N.J.).

Like the nonuniform, the paramilitary look is used only in a very specialized environment. The standard uniform is the police jumpsuit, boots, and utility belt (see Figure 8.4). This uniform is modeled on the police Special Weapons and Tactics (SWAT) team uniform and is used by strike forces, nuclear power plant guard forces, and other special units. It has a very harsh image and is generally inappropriate for most standard security work. An exception, however, is duty at sites such as landfills, construction yards, or manufacturing environments that would rapidly destroy a standard uniform or for which the standard uniform provides insufficient protection.

Figure 8.2 Traditional police style uniform (courtesy of Commercial Detective Agency, North Arlington, N.J.).

Selecting Uniforms

With the large variety of uniforms available, it is difficult for the guard company to choose a single style. Yet this is a critical decision in many ways. The uniformed guard is the direct representative of the company to the general public. The image he or she projects will be the one identified with the company. Selecting the wrong uniform for the market the guard company has targeted is fatal from a business standpoint. Uniforms that are not durable increase replacement costs. Those that provide insufficient environmental protection encourage guards to wear nonuniform clothing.

The first question that the guard company manager should ask is, Who are my clients? If the company markets solely to upscale corporate clients, then the standard uniform should be a suitable corporate style uniform. If the company does standard work that involves dealing with the criminal element, then the police style uniform should be the standard uniform.

In selecting the police style uniform as a standard, the company needs to

Figure 8.3 Corporate image uniform (courtesy of
Commercial Detective Agency, North Arlington,
N.J.).

consider how closely it wants the uniform to resemble the local police uniform. While this has been a practice in the security industry, it has been
largely discredited and may provide a liability exposure. Security guards are
not police officers and should not be mistaken for them. Several states have
laws governing the pattern and color of uniforms. For this reason, the use of
nonpolice colors and styles, such as contrasting pocket and epaulets is highly
recommended.

The same holds true for badges. Many security companies have com-

Figure 8.4   SWAT style uniform (courtesy of
Commercial Detective Agency, North Arlington, N.J.).

pletely eliminated the use of badges or have adopted simple cloth patches in
place of the badge. Cloth badges are particularly useful for wear on outer garments such as jackets and windbreakers because the guard is not required to
constantly switch his or her badge from shirt to outer garment and back
again. Another option is the use of plastic badges, which present a good appearance, do not damage uniform shirts, and are much cheaper than metal
badges. If a metal badge is used, it should not resemble a police badge. Again,
several states have laws regulating the use of badges.

Most guard companies adopt a shoulder patch bearing the company name and logo. Several states require that such a patch clearly identify the company as a guard company and not a public agency. The patch can also be used as a blazer crest. As with any item that reflects company image, the patch should be well designed and professionally sewn. While there are generic patches and badges available through uniform supply houses, they present a poor company image.

In addition to the standard uniform, the company may choose to offer optional uniforms to a potential client. For example, the company that uses a standard police style uniform may offer a blazer uniform as a special option. However, it is not cost-effective to offer too many different options and styles to a client. Every effort should be made to minimize the number of uniform components needed by the guard company. One way to do this is to design a standard uniform that could be worn either with or without a blazer. For example, a standard uniform of gray slacks and police style white shirt could be matched with either a black police jacket, a gray uniform jacket, or a navy blazer. Optional uniforms are normally billed to a client at a slightly higher rate than the standard uniform, since they involve additional expenditures on the part of the guard company.

Another question that should be asked is, Where do the guards work? The location of the company has an impact on the selection of uniforms. Most companies favor the use of polyester blends as they require little maintenance. However, polyester can be extremely uncomfortable in hot climates. Cotton might be more appropriate but wrinkles easily. Reputable uniform companies are usually familiar with local conditions and can offer advice on fabrics and blends appropriate to the company's needs.

Environmental protection can be a major uniform expense. Guards who perform outside tasks, such as patrol, vehicle inspections, or access control, must be provided with appropriate protective clothing such as jackets, hats, and raincoats. In locations where the weather is severe, the basic short police jacket is inappropriate—it tends to ride up and expose the wearer to drafts. Cowboy or trooper style hats with full brims offer more protection from sun and rain and are essential in areas such as the Southwest. Again, a little thought given to uniform design can significantly reduce cost. For example, a water-repellent jacket with a removable vest and liner can be used throughout the year, as opposed to a heavy jacket that can only be worn in winter.

Two other factors are essential in selecting a uniform: quality and cost. Unfortunately, these two must be balanced against each other. It is important for the company to select the best-quality uniforms it can afford. This involves making concessions. By limiting the number of options and uniform components, the company can keep costs down. Something as simple as eliminating a hat from the basic uniform or selecting adjustable baseball-type caps instead of sized police service hats can have a profound impact on uniform costs by reducing the need for an on-hand inventory of various sized hats. Details such as velcro on pocket flaps to prevent curling edges can make an inexpensive uniform look better than a more expensive one.

The proper uniform for a company, therefore, is one that is appropriate to the environment and the clients serviced by the guard company. The uniform should project a quality image for the company, yet offer substantial cost savings.

Obtaining Uniforms

There are a number of options available to the guard company for obtaining uniforms. The most common is for the company to maintain a stock of uniforms on hand and to issue uniform and equipment to the guard directly. This method allows the company to purchase uniforms in bulk at reduced prices and to maintain a level of control on the quality of the uniform issued. To be effective, however, this method requires that the company maintain an adequate supply of uniforms to meet projected and emergency needs, which requires a substantial capital investment. The company must arrange for cleaning and repair of uniforms and for replacement of worn-out or damaged items.

Rather than maintaining a stock of uniforms, some companies have opted to use a local uniform shop. New guards are sent to the uniform shop with a company purchase order. The guard is fitted for the appropriate uniform and the company is billed accordingly. The advantages to this approach are that the uniforms are new and tailored to the individual guard and the guard company does not have capital tied up in a uniform inventory. As guards leave, the uniforms are collected and form the nucleus of a company inventory. For these reasons, new companies often take this approach. The disadvantage to this method is that the cost per uniform is considerably higher than in a bulk purchase. In addition, since each new guard gets new uniforms, the overall cost for this method is extremely high.

A few companies require the guard to provide his or her own uniform, particularly when the standard uniform is very generic. Alternatively, the company may advance the guard the cost of uniforms through a purchase order to a local uniform shop, then deduct these costs from the guard's paycheck over a period of time. With this option, while the company has a very limited outlay for uniforms, it also has little or no control over the quality of uniform purchased. In addition, a terminated guard remains in control of a company uniform, creating a potential for misuse of the uniform in the commission of a crime.

There are a number of uniform companies who specialize in renting uniforms to organizations of different types. The rental contract specifies the type and quality of uniform and includes initial fitting and alteration, routine cleaning, and replacement of worn-out components. The cost, however, may be prohibitive for a guard company because of the rapid turnover endemic to the industry. It is, however, an extremely useful option to provide special uniforms to a particular client. For example, if the client requires a corporate style uniform in a particular color or fabric, the guard company can arrange to rent these uniforms through a uniform company and pass the costs directly to the client.

Uniform purchases should be approached in the same way a company makes any purchase. The company should identify qualified vendors and solicit proposals that are judged on their merits.

Equipment

Depending on the nature of a guard's duties, the company may need to provide basic equipment for the guard. Obviously, any equipment added to the basic issue list increases the overall uniform expense to the company. Consequently, only those items absolutely necessary to the performance of duty should be provided.

There are items that the guard can be expected to provide. However, any requirements to provide items must be spelled out clearly in the company's general orders. Generally, the guard can be expected to provide generic items such as a notebook, pen, pencil, flashlight, and spare batteries. The guard manager must also realize that he or she has little control over the quality of the items provided by the guard. For example, the company can require the guard to provide a flashlight but cannot force the guard to purchase a particular make and model.

Each item provided by the company carries a certain inherent liability. For example, if the company provides handcuffs, it must also provide training on both the appropriate physical techniques used in applying handcuffs and the circumstances under which they may be used. Issuing first aid packets or pocket airways implies that the guard can give first aid and that proper training has been provided.

If the guard has been provided with a good standard uniform and clearly understands those items that he or she must provide, the only specialized equipment that needs to be issued should be site-specific. For example, the contract may call for the guard on a particular post to carry a chemical protective spray, baton, and handcuffs. Another post may require safety shoes and a jumpsuit. Note that these items are regarded as individual equipment required by the guard, not post equipment, which will be dealt with below.

Issuing Uniforms and Equipment

For the average guard company, the most cost-effective solution for uniforms will be to maintain an inventory. This inventory represents a substantial investment and must be safeguarded, which means maintaining accurate records of issue, turned-in items, stock on hand, items on order, items received, and items discarded as unserviceable.

As items are purchased, they should be added to a master inventory list maintained by the accounting department. Items that have been lost, have been damaged beyond repair, or have reached the end of their useful life are removed from the master list. Lost or damaged equipment should be accounted for through a formal reporting process (Figure 8.5) that allows the company to fix fiscal responsibility for the loss. The guard company should have a clear policy on how loss is accounted for and under what circumstances the guard is expected to reimburse the company for the loss.

The basic tool of the inventory clerk is an issue record for each guard (Figure 8.6), which records company property that has been issued to the guard and that must be returned to the company upon termination. Note that it allows for the issuance of new or additional items or for the turning in of unneeded items. By counting the items on these issue records and counting the stock on hand, the inventory clerk should be able to account for all items on the master inventory list. The clerk's supervisor should conduct such an inventory at least annually.

The company must provide the inventory clerk with basic guidelines as to the number and type of items to issue. These should include both a basic issue list applicable to all guards and post-specific lists. For example, a guard assigned to a truck gate requiring outside inspection of incoming vehicles would receive a basic issue plus a raincoat or overcoat, hat, and flashlight. A guard in a manufacturing plant may receive a basic issue plus safety shoes and a hardhat.

In addition to signing an inventory sheet, many companies also require that a guard provide a uniform deposit. This deposit is used to ensure the return of the uniform in serviceable condition and may be used for any additional cleaning and repair required. The deposit is generally not sufficient to cover replacement of the entire uniform, which may cost several hundred dollars, but it does provide an incentive for the guard to return the uniform upon termination. The deposit may be collected through a series of payroll deductions. The deposit, less cleaning costs, if any, is returned to the guard after the uniforms have been returned to the company. While some states have laws forbidding the collection of uniform deposits, it should be part of any uniform-recovery program wherever possible.

The guard company should be aggressive in recovering uniforms both because of the cost involved and because of the image problem that could be generated by misuse of a company uniform. The cost of uniform items can, in most cases, be deducted from a guard's final paycheck. However, most states will not allow the guard's paycheck to be withheld until the uniform is

REPORT OF DAMAGE TO OR LOSS OF UNIFORM OR EQUIPMENT

1. COMPLAINT NUMBER			2. TYPE OF REPORT ☐ LOST ☐ STOLEN ☐ DAMAGED
3. EMPLOYEE'S NAME LAST, FIRST, MIDDLE	4. BADGE	5. ORG. ELEMENT	6. WAS EMPLOYEE ON DUTY OR OFF DUTY ☐ ON DUTY ☐ OFF DUTY
7. DESCRIPTION OF PROPERTY		8. ACQ. VALUE	9. DATE STOLEN, LOST OR DAMAGED
			10. DATE AND TIME WHEN LAST SEEN
			11. LOCATION WHERE LAST SEEN
			12. WHERE REGULARLY STORED
			13. SUPERVISOR INCIDENT FIRST REPORTED TO

14. STATEMENT OF FACTS: DETAIL THE CIRCUMSTANCES SURROUNDING THE LOSS, DAMAGE OR THEFT AND THE ACTION TAKEN TO RECOVER THE PROPERTY OR VALUE THEREOF. BE BRIEF, CONCISE AND ACCURATE.

15. I CERTIFY THE FOREGOING STATEMENT TO BE TRUE AND COMPLETE ACCORDING TO MY BEST KNOWLEDGE AND RECOLLECTION.

DATE   EMPLOYEE'S SIGNATURE

Figure 8.5   Uniform loss report. [From Guy et al., *Forms for Safety and Security Management.* (Boston: Butterworth Publishers, 1981.)]

INDIVIDUAL EQUIPMENT LISTING

NAME: _____ BADGE NO. _____
            (Last,   First,   M.I.)

SIGNATURE: _____ LAST INVENTORY DATE: _____
                                                              (Pencil Entry)

ITEM	AMOUNT	DATE	RE-ISSUES INITIAL	DATE	INITIAL	REMARKS
Badge						
Badge, Cap						
Braid, Gold, Supervisor						
Belt, Garrison						
Belt, Sam Browne w/two (2) Keepers						
Blouse, Security						
Gloves, Leather						
Hat, Pile, Fur Trooper						
Hat, Security (male)						
Hat, Security (female)						
Holster, Pistol, Leather						
Jacket, Winter, Tuffy Topper						
Nametag, Plastic						
Nightstick, w/Grommet & Lazy Strap						
Restraint, Metal (handcuff)						
Restraint, Case Leather						
Ring, Key w/Pocket Protector						
Shirts, Blue						
Shirts, White						
Skirt						
Tie, Clasp, Metal						
Tie, Neck, Black (male)						
Tie, Neck, Black (female)						
Trouser, Black						
Whistle, Plastic w/Chain & Holder						

Figure 8.6 Individual issue record. [From Guy et al., *Forms for Safety and Security Management*. (Boston: Butterworth Publishers, 1981.)]

returned. Consequently, the company may need to send a supervisor to collect the uniforms or seek a civil remedy through small claims court.

An aggressive uniform recovery program should have several components:

1. The guard must be made aware during orientation and periodically afterwards that he or she has an obligation to return all company property upon termination.
2. All company property issued to the guard must be acknowledged by the guard's signature on an issue document.
3. Wherever possible, a uniform deposit should be collected from the guard.
4. The cost of the unreturned uniform (or as much as possible) should be deducted from the guard's final paycheck, if allowed by law.
5. A certified, return-receipt letter should be sent to the guard demanding the return of the uniform by a certain date.
6. A representative of the guard company should attempt to collect the uniforms in person.
7. The former employee should be sued in small claims court.

Post Equipment

A client contract may call for the use of special equipment at a specific post. This equipment may be provided by the client, may be purchased by the guard company at the client's request, or may be purchased by the guard company and loaned to the client. Examples of this type of equipment are tour clocks, radios, flashlights, and safety equipment such as hardhats.

All this property must be carefully safeguarded. The post orders for a specific post should contain a list of equipment assigned to the post. Using a standard inventory list (Figure 8.7), each incoming guard is then expected to check that the items are on hand as required. Any missing equipment must be reported immediately to the guard's supervisor. This is particularly important in the case of expensive client equipment that will involve substantial replacement costs.

Assigning equipment to a post rather than to individuals has several significant advantages to the guard company. It reduces the amount of equipment issued to individual guards and, consequently, reduces cost. For example, issuing one good-quality flashlight to each post is much cheaper than issuing flashlights to each guard in the company. It is also easier to apportion costs to be billed to the client.

A disadvantage is that responsibility for the equipment is not fixed with a specific individual. Consequently, missing or unserviceable equipment may

SECURITY DEPARTMENT
EQUIPMENT CHECK LIST

OFFICE

7	TWO WAY RADIOS	( )
8	SPARE RADIO BATTERIES	( )
2	TIME CLOCKS WITH CASES	( )
1	CO_2 FIRE EXTINGUISHER	( )
1	WATER FIRE EXTINGUISHER	( )
3	RAINCOATS	( )
4	WRIST RESTRAINTS	( )
2	ANKLE RESTRAINTS	( )
1	POST KEY	( )
2	RESTRICTED AREA SIGNS	( )
6	WINTER COATS	( )
2	SETS OF KEYS WITH GRAND MASTER & SECURITY MASTER EACH	( )
2	SYSTEM 7 CARDS (UNRESTRICTED)	( )
	CHECK KEY CABINET (LOCKED)	( )
5	A. R. A. KEYS (NO. 1-2-3-4-5)	( )
6	FLASHLIGHTS	( )
2	HALON FIRE EXTINGUISHERS	( )

BOOTH

30	SECURITY PASSES	( )
1	FLASHLIGHT	( )
2	DRY CHEMICAL EXTINGUISHERS	( )
1	RAINCOAT	( )
1	CLIPBOARD	( )
2	LOCKS	( )
1	SET OF KEYS TO BOOTH	( )
1	GATE RADIO RADIO CONTROL	( )

DATE _____ SHIFT _____ TIME _____

I VERIFY THAT I HAVE CHECKED ALL OF THE ABOVE ITEMS AND SAME HAVE BEEN ACCOUNTED FOR EXCEPT:

_____
_____
_____
_____

(SIGNATURE OF DESK OFFICER)

Figure 8.7 Post equipment inventory sheet. [From Guy et al., *Forms for Safety and Security Management.* (Boston: Butterworth Publishers, 1981.)]

not be reported for several shift changes or until discovered by a supervisor, making it difficult to fix financial responsibility for the loss. Supervisors must make an inventory of post equipment during any inspection and discipline any guard who fails to report damaged or missing equipment.

Vehicle Budgets

A guard company has an inherent need for transportation. Managers must meet with clients; supervisors must inspect posts. Many companies meet this need by allowing the reimbursed use of private vehicles. This reimbursement is treated as an expense by the accounting function. Where the company has leased or purchased a patrol vehicle, however, there is a need for an operating budget for vehicles, separate from the lease/purchase account.

The vehicle operating budget addresses several key items. The cost of fuel and oil is the most obvious, and unfortunately, this is as far as most guard companies go. A realistic budget must include an estimate for repairs and for routine servicing and maintenance, unless included in the lease. The need for this is readily apparent. Like a police patrol vehicle, the guard patrol vehicle will be in almost constant use. It will be subjected to a high degree of stress and will be routinely exposed to heavy traffic and unsafe road conditions, such as snow or rain. To continue to function properly, it must receive routine, periodic maintenance. If possible, these costs should be built into the lease. Where they are not, they must be budgeted for.

Maintenance for the guard vehicle should be scheduled by mileage rather than by time. This is because the amount of miles driven in a particular time period is a variable and will normally exceed the manufacturer's time projections. Because of this frequent need for servicing, it is recommended that the company have an additional vehicle available to allow the patrol vehicle to be taken out of service. This additional vehicle can be either a regular patrol vehicle that has been purchased or leased or a rental vehicle provided under a regular contract. To contract for patrol work without making provisions for backup vehicles is poor management.

Vehicle budgeting revolves around an estimated annual mileage figure, developed by the operations section based on the expected patrol patterns and areas. As an alternative, the planner can use a rough estimate based on average speed. For example, if the standard patrol speed for the company is 15 mph, the planner can assume a 24-hour, 365-day operation for a total annual mileage of 131,400 miles. This high figure is then reduced by eliminating hours that the vehicle will be known to be out of service. The planner should make assumptions similar to the following:

1. The vehicle will not be used for three hours per day during shift changes.

2. The driver will spend six hours a day on foot patrol and routine inspections.
3. The vehicle will be unavailable for fourteen days a year for repair and servicing.

Using these assumptions, the annual mileage in this example drops to 78,975 miles. Bear in mind that these are planning estimates only and that, as the company accumulates data from actual experience, these figures will become more accurate.

Once an annual mileage is estimated, other costs begin to fall into place. For example, if the vehicle is to be serviced every 7,500 miles, the estimated 78,975 miles of operation will require at least ten services at a cost of $30 each. A major tune up will normally be needed every 30,000 miles; this estimate requires two at $80 each. Fuel costs are calculated on the basis of the vehicle's miles-per-gallon rating. Assuming an average of 20 mpg, this estimate requires 3,949 gallons of fuel at $1.20 a gallon.

Repair costs are difficult to estimate and are projected best when based on historical records. Major vehicular damage will be handled by insurance, but there is a need to consider the deductible and the many small things that go wrong with a vehicle. In the absence of any data, this example will use $1,200—the company's deductible plus 20 percent.

All these costs are then added to obtain the total vehicle-operating budget for the year: $6,399. The budget is then apportioned out over the twelve-month period, giving a monthly budget of $533. Note that a change in any of the variables just discussed can raise or lower this figure. If estimates are used, as was done here, they should be revised as soon as hard data is developed.

9

Training

The key to good customer service is training. Guards cannot be expected to perform well unless they have been taught what constitutes acceptable performance. Unfortunately, while many guard companies profess to offer trained guards, few have the type of comprehensive program needed to provide quality performance. The most common reason given for this lack is the cost associated with training. Yet the cost of poor training can be higher: lost contracts and lawsuits. Training does not have to be expensive to be good.

The secret of a good training program is continuity—the progressive and continuous reinforcement of company standards. Progressive training means that each level of the company, from entry-level to senior management, must have identified training goals. These goals should build on and reinforce previous training and, ideally, reflect expanded responsibility that comes with longevity of service.

A progressive training program can be divided into several levels: *preassignment* training, *site-specific* training, *sustainment* training, *supervisory* training, and *management* training.

Motivation

Any student tends to take training more seriously if he or she can see some immediate and tangible benefit. Consequently, training, particularly sustainment training (discussed later) should be tied to a system of rewards. One way of doing this is to determine various step levels for guards and tie the completion of certain types of training to promotions and salary increases. As a guard progresses through the various training levels, he or she is preparing for eventual promotion as a supervisor. While not all guards will be able to meet the standards for supervisors, the general quality of the guard force will be significantly improved by having tangible rewards for training.

Consideration should also be given to developing a long-term benefit for the guard if training is satisfactorily completed. The John Buck Company of Chicago developed a training program for the company's proprietary guards. The curriculum was submitted to the Illinois Community College Board, and the course was accredited. Guards completing the course received certificates from the company's sponsoring educational institution (Villarreal, 1994, p. 65).

Documenting Training

A critical part of any training program is the ability of the company to prove that training has been provided. This documentation must include *who* was trained and *what* was taught. This information may become critical in a lawsuit and can prove either that a guard was acting properly or that he or she was acting outside the scope of employment.

To adequately document training, the company should maintain individual training records and a master training file.

Individual Training Records

Individual records are filed in the guard's personnel folder and must include the dates and the subject covered. The easiest way is to issue a company certificate for any training provided (Figure 9.1). These are easily produced by using a computer-based program or by purchasing stock certificates at an office supply outlet. Certificates that are awarded frequently, such as at completion of preassignment training, can be preprinted in bulk. The certificate serves two purposes: it can be easily copied and filed in the guard's personnel file, and it provides the guard with a permanent record of training that can be used in future job applications.

If the company has a truly progressive and formalized training program, it is also possible to use a single record sheet that is annotated after each training session is completed (Figure 9.2). This has the advantage of providing a quick summary of the guard's level of training. However, it is labor-intensive to pull the guard's file each time he or she receives training.

A third method of keeping individual records is to use a computer database system. Several of the guard scheduling programs discussed in chapter 6

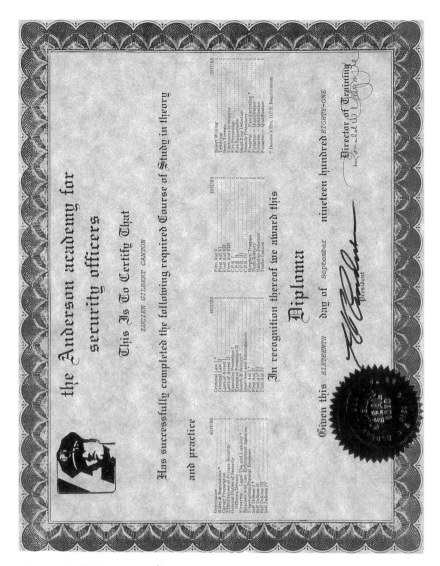

Figure 9.1   Training certificate.

include modules that track personnel qualifications and training. This allows the company to print summaries of both individual and company training status. For example, the computer can produce the names of all guards who have completed a supervisor training course when the company is looking to promote a new supervisor. It can also provide monthly listings of guards who are due for requalification training for first aid or firearms certificates.

One type of training that is critical to schedulers and dispatchers is site-

INDIVIDUAL TRAINING RECORD				
NAME:_____ EMPLOYEE #_____				
SUBJECT	HOURS	GRADE	DATE	INSTRUCTOR'S INITIALS
Orientation	2			
Legal Powers	2			
Handling Emergencies	2			
General Duties	2			

Figure 9.2   Individual training record.

specific training. This is normally on-the-job training that qualifies a guard to work a specific client site. A list of guards trained on a particular site can be extremely useful to a dispatcher trying to fill an open shift. It can prevent client complaints by providing a trained replacement rather than just a "warm body." Such a list can be easily generated through a computer database if the company has developed a method for site supervisors to report this type of training.

Individual training records should also include training and experience that the guard has previously received before joining the company. This could serve to fill in any gaps in training in the event of a lawsuit. In addition, it avoids penalizing an experienced guard who is new to the company for not taking company training that might be required for promotion or assignment.

Company Training Records

Training is a double-edged sword in some ways. If it is not provided, the company can be liable for negligence. If it is provided, however, the company may need to prove that it is adequate and appropriate. For this reason, the company needs to maintain records on all training that has been provided to the guard.

The file on a particular training session must contain two items: a lesson plan and a class roster. The lesson plan may be either an outline or a manuscript, but it should be sufficiently detailed to demonstrate the specific topics covered (Figure 9.3). Wherever possible, lessons should be based on nationally recognized standards or references that can be used to defend the subject matter included in the session. If instructor certifications are required, they should be on file in the instructor's personnel folder. An advantage to certification is that the certifying body is normally prepared to assist in the legal defense of an instructor by providing information and expert witnesses on the subject in question. If contractors are used to provide training, their qualifications should be included with their proposals and filed.

Background material used by the instructor should also be part of the lesson file. This includes handouts, tests, and copies of visual aids. Video tapes

---

TRAINING OUTLINE

SUBJECT: Handling Emergencies

TIME REQUIRED: 4 Hours

REFERENCES: Instructor's notes

TRAINING AIDS: Fire Extinguisher Video
                        Earthquake Video

LESSON OUTLINE

OBJECTIVE: To familiarize the guard with emergencies that could occur on the guard's assigned site and the role of the guard force in dealing with them.

I. Fire Emergencies

    a. Basic Fire Chemistry

    b. Origins of fires and prevention

    c. Classification of fires and equipment

    d. Fire alarm system

    e. Fire supression system

    f. Fire response and evacuation

II. Earthquake

    a. Earthquake scenarios

    b. Pre-quake safety patrol

    c. Earthquake response

    d. Recovery

III. Miscellaneous emergencies

    a. power outages

    b. bomb threats

    c. floods

Figure 9.3   Training outline.

prepared for the security or law enforcement industries generally are accompanied by instructor guides, which should also be filed.

There are two approaches to lesson files. If the program is standardized, there is no need to maintain a separate folder for each time the class is taught. Class rosters can be filed separately from the lesson file. If the training session changes or is a one-time session, then there should be a separate lesson file for each session. Backup material and references need not be duplicated each time but can be filed in a separate reference folder.

A good training session includes a test that demonstrates whether the guard has understood the subject matter. These tests may be filed with the lesson file or included in the guard's personnel folder, the preferred location. However, if the guard fails a test and the company takes no corrective action or fails to demonstrate that corrective action through a retest, these facts can be readily used to prove negligence on the part of the company.

Preassignment Training

Training Topics

Preassignment training, also referred to as *entry-level* or *initial orientation*, is training given to a guard prior to his or her first assignment with the guard company. The goal for this type of training is to provide the guard with an understanding of the basic information he or she will need on the job. The most important part of this training is a thorough explanation of company standards contained in the company's general orders handbook.

The length of this type of training is a subject of heated discussion among guard company managers. The Task Force on Private Security recommended a minimum of eight hours (Figure 9.4), to be followed by a minimum of thirty-two hours within three months, with no more than sixteen hours to be on-the-job training. However, *The Hallcrest Report* (Cunningham and Taylor, 1985) found that the average guard received only four hours of training and that sixty percent of the contract guards surveyed received only on-the-job training.

In determining the appropriate number of hours for an initial training course, the company must ask the question, What do we need to teach the new guard? There is a tendency to try to overwhelm a new employee by teaching all the things that he or she will need to know as a security guard. This is an impossible task, in terms of time, cost, and the ability of a student to retain information. So the company must determine the minimum number of subjects that must be covered and the time required for each one.

Some subjects are automatically included in any orientation. The first section should be on company standards and should emphasize dismissable offenses and standards for conduct and appearance. It should also include the

---

Model Preassignment Training Program
for a Guard or Watchman

Section I   **Orientation (2 hours)**

	Minutes
- What is security?	15
- Public relations	15
- Deportment	15
- Appearance	10
- Maintenance and safeguarding of uniforms and/or equipment	20
- Note taking/reporting	15
- Role of public law enforcement	10

Section II   **Legal Powers and Limitations (2 hours)**

- Prevention versus apprehension	40
- Use of force	25
- Search and seizure	15
- Arrest powers	20

Section III   **Handling Emergencies (2 hours)**

- Procedures for bomb threats	40
- Procedures during fires, explosions, floods, riots, and so forth	60

Section IV   **General Duties (2 hours)**

- Patrol	40
- Fire prevention and control	30
- Safety	30

Figure 9.4   Task Force on Private Security model training program. This schedule allows for a ten-minute break each hour.

company's standards for dealing with clients and reinforce the company's commitment to client service.

The second critical topic is the civil and criminal laws pertinent to the guard's work. This does not mean that the guard must learn every violation that might be encountered on duty and the legal elements of proof for each crime. Rather, it should focus on the legal limits of the guard's authority. Of particular concern are the topics of powers of arrest and use of force. These two subjects, more than any others, tend to land security guards in court.

The section on law should be tailored to the guard's actual role. For example, if the company specializes in retail security, the legal section will be lengthy and include laws on shoplifting and theft. If the company has a no-arrest policy, this portion will be very short.

A third critical section is an explanation of how the guard is to handle emergencies. Again, this does not have to be extremely detailed unless the company has a particular specialization that warrants more extensive coverage. The intent of this section is to tell a new employee what to do or who to call if something goes wrong.

Most companies include a section on observation, note taking, and report writing, all important subjects that should be introduced in the initial training session. However, in the limited time available in orientation, it is unlikely that the guard will emerge as an experienced investigator. These topics must form part of sustainment training and be continuously reinforced. The focus should be on basic requirements and how to get help with these subjects.

Optional subjects are again tailored to the company. For example, if the guard is issued handcuffs, the company must provide instruction on their use. If the guard is armed, firearms training must be conducted. If the guard is expected to fight small fires, basic training on the use of fire extinguishers must be provided. The rule of thumb is that any action or piece of equipment that the guard is expected to be able to perform or use *immediately* upon assignment must be explained; subjects that can be handled as on-the-job or sustainment training may be deferred.

Training Options

Because initial training is one of the few times that a guard will be available for formal training, most guard companies tend to make full use of packaged training programs. These provide consistent and interesting training to the candidates and reduce the requirement for instructor involvement. A member of the office staff can open each session, start the program, then return to his or her duties until it is complete. The instructor then answers questions and performs any testing required.

The best packaged programs are those designed specifically for the individual guard company, either as slide presentations or as videos. Unfortunately, only large companies can usually afford to do these. If the guard company decides to produce its own materials, slide shows are fairly easy to produce. They can also be easily updated. Video production is much more dynamic but is also much more difficult and expensive. In either case, use a production consultant. Amateur videos have no place in initial training where the emphasis is on building the employee's commitment to the guard company.

Several companies, such as Motorola Teleprograms, Inc., offer slide programs that can be enhanced by company-specific slides, allowing the instructor to use actual client sites and personnel in company uniforms in the presentation. Modifying these packages offers an inexpensive alternative to producing a proprietary program.

There are also several companies that offer video programs in either a generic or industry-specific format. For example, Communicorp, Inc., offers training programs geared to the hospital security industry. The Professional Security Television Network (PSTN) produces modular training programs for basic and in-service guard training, as well as training programs for supervisors and managers. PSTN also provides a video library service that allows the guard company to tailor sustainment training to match its current needs.

Reducing Training Costs

Initial training costs are primarily in the area of employee salaries. If the guard candidate is an employee, he or she must be paid for training time. Several companies get around this by making the completion of initial orientation training a condition for employment. The candidate must attend and successfully complete this training before being offered employment. This allows the company to weed out those who cannot pass training before locking them in as employees and removes the requirement for paying wages to the candidate.

A second option is to pay new guards a training wage for a specified period of time, such as thirty days or until completion of initial and site-specific training. While this does not eliminate costs, it does reduce them. It also projects a better image of the company than not paying any wages for training.

A company can also reduce initial training costs by requiring a certain amount of pretraining. In California, for example, it is not uncommon for a company to require a guard to have state certification before applying for a job. The possession of such certification is taken as evidence that the guard is aware of his or her legal status and the laws of arrest, search, and seizure. This not only reduces the length of training but also saves the company the cost of the state certification fee.

Several companies have taken this a step further by establishing company training academies that will train and certify guard candidates for a fee. The academy is usually a separate financial entity, and the fee is charged back to the parent company. The training costs are then allocated to general overhead, and the guard company does not actually conduct any training. Candidates attending the academy are generally not paid. Vocational schools and community colleges sometimes offer similar training and are eager to place graduates in order to maintain federal funding. It is possible to arrange a recruiting program with such a school in lieu of providing extensive orientation training. However, the level of quality of these programs varies greatly, and the curriculum and instructors' qualifications should be periodically reviewed by the guard company.

A major drawback to using prequalification or outside agencies such as vocational schools in lieu of initial training is the lack of quality control. The guard company has no way of knowing if all required subjects were covered or how well they were taught. While these options do offer some cost reductions, in the long term, they are no substitute for a company-developed and company-controlled training program. If the guard company elects to use prequalification or outside training agencies to reduce costs, the company must put in place some method of checking on the applicant's job knowledge and level of training, such as a preemployment skills test. The use of prequalification or outside training does not substantially lessen the guard company's legal responsibility for providing adequate training.

Performance-Based Training

Traditional training relies on the development of a curriculum and the presentation of the curriculum subjects to the trainee in a formal training setting. This is not always the most effective training method for a guard company. Instead, many companies have been experimenting with performance-based programs in which training is built around specific tasks that the guard must actually perform. After demonstrating an acceptable level of skill in the task, the guard is rated as qualified in that task and can progress to another.

A major benefit of performance-based training is that it measures training effectiveness before the guard is considered qualified. The task must be demonstrated and meet a clearly identified training standard. This system is used very effectively by the military to teach required skills. Performance-based training forces the trainer to identify the essential tasks that must be performed by the guard and the acceptable performance standards. This tends to focus training and eliminate superfluous information. Performance-based training is particularly applicable to on-the-job training.

Unfortunately, not all subjects lend themselves well to performance-based training. Some subjects, such as legal authorities, require lengthy explanations and examples. Even with these subjects, however, it may be possible to make the training more effective through the use of scenarios.

Site-Specific Training

Once the guard has been equipped with the knowledge needed to perform basic duties, he or she must be trained for the specific job location where he or she will be assigned. While guard duties tend to be fairly similar at all locations, each client has unique requirements that must be met by the guard. Each location has a different physical layout and a different corporate culture. The duties of a guard in a high-rise office building are substantially different from those of a guard at a construction site, even though both are conducting patrols and checking identification. The goal of site-specific training is to adequately prepare the guard to perform all tasks required by the contract for the client's location. Consequently, training should be performance-based rather than knowledge-based.

"Training" usually conjures up an image of a classroom where an instructor lectures to seated students who take notes. Few client sites require this type of formal instruction. Instead, the requirement is usually for one or two guards to be trained on specific duties. This means that training is generally delivered as a specific form of performance-based training known as on-the-job training. On-the-job-training is the most common form of site-specific training in the guard industry and also the most poorly handled. There is a tendency to assume that because a guard has been briefed on a post by a supervisor or has worked a shift with another guard, he or she has been trained to work that location. There is rarely any test of the guard's ability to perform the contract-mandated tasks. To be effective, on-the-job training must be structured, supervised, and consistent with company standards.

The foundation for site-specific training is the post orders. These instructions should contain all the basics that a guard needs to know for properly carrying out his or her duties at the site (see chapter 6, "Operations"). From the post orders, it is possible to develop a checklist of training tasks that must be mastered by the guard (Figure 9.5). The checklist includes the training objective and the date it was explained and demonstrated to the guard by the trainer. The next column provides the date when the guard satisfactorily performed the task. Once the checklist is complete, the supervisor signs off on it and forwards it to the personnel section for filing in the guard's personnel folder. The guard is then considered qualified to work that particular post.

Reducing Training Costs

New guards should undergo a probationary period, during which it is assumed that the guard is still learning about the company and the client site. Consequently, he or she may be paid a training wage until the probationary period ends. The cost savings can be justified as necessary to offset the costs of increased supervision and the need to staff the post with both a trained guard and the trainee.

The amount of time required for site-specific training is based on either a period mandated by the contract or the guard manager's estimate. Contract

---

On-the-Job Training Record

Guard: _____

Post: _____

Completion
Date: _____

Task	Date Explained To Guard	Date Demonstrated By Guard	Trainer
1. Knows location of all fire extinguishers Post Orders, p. 5			
2. Knows emergency contact numbers Post Orders, p. 1			
3. Knows patrol route Post Checklist			

Figure 9.5 Training checklist.

minimums usually allow no adjustment for previous experience. Wherever possible, the guard company manager should attempt to build in a certain amount of flexibility. If a guard is clearly able to perform all the training tasks on the training checklist, training time can be waived or reduced. This allows experienced guards to move to a new site without incurring the full training costs generated by a new employee. The company should, however, establish a minimum training time for all posts to avoid abuse of this system.

Sustainment Training

In a professional guard company, training never ends. Guards should continually receive refresher training in basic subjects and be kept abreast of changes both in the company and in the guard industry. The goal of this ongoing training, known as *sustainment training*, is to provide professional development opportunities to long-term employees.

The core subjects for sustainment training should be basic security topics to expand the guard's knowledge beyond the minimum required in preassignment training and to reinforce essential skills not used regularly in day-to-day activities. Sustainment training can also provide refresher training on company standards and policies or explain new procedures.

Sustainment training rarely involves formal classroom training. Instead, it relies on interaction between the supervisor and the individual guard. Consequently, sustainment training can be viewed as possessing two components: one, consisting of training provided by the company, and another, consisting of training encouraged by the company.

There are several methods of providing continuing training. A simple system used by many companies is to prepare a monthly training bulletin on a specific training topic. This bulletin includes a written test that must be completed by the guard and turned in to the supervisor for grading. Guards who fail the test receive on-the-spot corrective training from the supervisor until they master the topic. Tests are then filed in the employees' personnel folders.

At least one company provides a hotline with prerecorded training messages that change each month. The guard calls the hotline, listens to the message, then takes a brief test provided by the supervisor. The supervisor provides immediate feedback and training to those guards who cannot initially pass the test.

As in any on-the-job training program, the role of the supervisor is critical. The supervisor provides feedback that reinforces the learned skills. He or she can provide explanation of unclear points. The commitment of the supervisor to training mirrors the commitment of the company. Note that using a test allows the supervisor to focus on those guards who are having trouble with a specific training topic, rather than requiring him or her to spend the same amount of time on each guard.

Correspondence courses have been the mainstay of distance education for many years. However, until recently, there were few that were suitable for security guards. Many are of the "matchbook" school of correspondence study and are not worth the investment of time or money. One excellent option for the guard, however, is the Certified Protection Officer (CPO) program offered by the International Foundation for Protection Officers. Candidates must have six months of experience, be recommended by two security professionals, and complete a self-paced course of study that includes a mid-term and proctored final examination. Successful graduates are awarded the CPO certification.

Other certification programs exist that the guard company may want to encourage employees to take. The most inexpensive and most useful are the first aid and CPR programs offered by the American Red Cross. There may also be other programs offered by various public agencies, such as the police and fire departments.

Another avenue for encouraging professional development, particularly for supervisors and entry-level managers, is a tuition- reimbursement program in which the company agrees to pay all or a portion of the educational costs incurred by the guard, provided that the program is approved in advance and that the guard graduates successfully. The state of California, for example, offers its Fire Safety Director Course (a state-developed course focusing on high-rise building fire safety) through the community college system. The community college system also offers reserve police officer training that is directly applicable to a security guard's duties. However, while a tuition-reimbursement program is very worthwhile, the costs involved may be too high for a small company.

There are numerous options for sustainment training. However, merely making these opportunities available does not meet the needs of the guard company. There must be a commitment on the part of management to encourage and reward employees for participating in such a program. Further, management must oversee such training to ensure that it is relevant and cost-effective. Like on-the-job training, a program of sustainment training must be carefully laid out with well-defined goals.

Supervisor Training

A primary function of the guard supervisor is to conduct sustainment training. Therefore, guards selected for promotion to supervisory positions should have mastered the basics of their profession. However, mastery of basic skills does not completely prepare a guard for his or her role of supervisor. The interpersonal and professional skills needed can be quite different from those required of even a lead guard. The goal of supervisor training, therefore, is to teach the necessary supervisory skills.

Effective supervisor training programs offer both professional development and supervisory training. The professional-development training increases the supervisor's knowledge of the security profession by providing more detailed instruction than he or she received as a guard. For example, while guards are taught the basic components of an alarm system, the supervisor may be introduced to the theories behind developing alarm systems. The guard needs to know how to use a tour-management system; the supervisor needs to know how to develop a guard tour. This in-depth knowledge of basic skills is a fundamental requisite for the supervisor's role as trainer.

Although a guard should develop the ability to deal with people through work experience, a supervisory position requires different and more extensive communication skills. A supervisor can expect increased client contact, usually because a problem has developed on the site. How he or she handles these contacts will have a direct bearing on client retention. The supervisor can also expect to play an increased role in marketing, as he or she is likely to be approached by potential clients seeking information about the guard company. The new supervisor will also be expected to deal with guards on a different level from what he or she is used to—the supervisor must now provide counseling, discipline, and training.

The most demanding problem for the supervisor will be the transition from guard to supervisor, a difficult change for even the most qualified candidate. To ease the transition, it is important that management clearly demonstrate confidence in the supervisor through personal contact and company-wide announcements. Preassignment training should be provided before the supervisor begins his or her first shift. Ideally, this training should have been through an advanced sustainment training course open to selected guards.

It is a mistake to assume that a new supervisor understands the basics of motivational theory or knows how to conduct a counseling session. He or she will also need to fully understand the company's disciplinary system and those personnel laws and regulations that apply to his or her duties.

The amount of administrative training required by the supervisor will depend on the role played by the supervisor in the guard company. If the supervisor is responsible for preparing payroll information, then this is a logical training topic. If he or she merely turns in time sheets without processing, then the training required is significantly reduced. If the supervisor handles scheduling or fills empty shifts, he or she needs to have an understanding of operations and costs.

One of the best ways for a supervisor to learn the guard business is to provide him or her with an opportunity to spend time in the company office. Unlike a guard who is committed to a single client site, supervisors can sometimes be scheduled to spend a certain period of time each month in the company office. This allows them to be trained directly by the administrative and operations staff and to gain experience in these areas by taking on simple projects. This system can also provide a pool of trained replacements for office staff during vacation periods and potential promotion opportunities for the supervisor.

Because supervisors can be expected to visit the office on a regular basis, it is possible to make better use of additional training options, such as videotape programs and the Professional Security Television Network. A topic for the month, possibly tied in with the topic for sustainment training, is selected and appropriate videos rented. The supervisor then takes a few moments at some point during the month to view the video and take the quiz associated with it. There are several programs available that offer short, concise videos of five minutes, suitable for viewing prior to or just after a shift. Many videos on security topics are no more than twenty minutes long, allowing the supervisor to complete a training module in thirty minutes or less.

The supervisor is entering a level of professional development in which seminars on supervision and security management might be useful. While there are few seminars for security guards that deal with nontactical issues, the guard company should encourage attendance at professional-level seminars addressing supervision and management whenever possible.

Managerial Training

Management-Training Programs

Like guards, managers need both entry-level and sustainment training. Unfortunately, too many guard companies hire entry-level managers with no experience in the guard industry and provide only on-the-job training. This means that the manager learns by trial and error (mostly by error). It is critical that entry-level managers undergo formal training designed to provide them with a basic understanding of the guard business. Even managers with considerable experience as guards may not really understand the business side of the guard company.

The simplest way to provide management training is to rotate the manager through various company positions. If the manager has no prior guard experience, this rotation should include time on a guard post and as a field supervisor. Key office staff should serve as trainers. Just as in the guards' on-the-job training program, each of these trainers should have a checklist that covers all the tasks that the management trainee must master. A senior member of management should be appointed to oversee training and to serve as a mentor to the management trainee.

Most new managers spend considerable time in operations. This is only natural, as it is the heart of the business. However, without a solid understanding of how contracts are developed by the marketing function and how costs are allocated by the accounting function, an entry-level manager is usually no more effective than a supervisor. It is the ability to see beyond the current operational problem and to see how it affects sales and profits that distinguishes the manager from the supervisor.

In addition to formal on-the-job training, the management trainee should also be required to read professional publications such as *Security Management* and *Security* magazines. A selected reading list of security books dealing with the guard industry should also be provided to the trainee. These books are readily available through public libraries or from professional libraries such as the one maintained by the American Society for Industrial Security. The guard company should also develop its own reading file with company-specific information. The required reading list for a management trainee should also include the company policy and procedures manual and the standards of conduct booklet issued to the guards.

Management trainees should be encouraged to join professional organizations. These are not limited to security organizations but might also include organizations peculiar to the company's client base. Such memberships provide invaluable information and foster the development of professional contacts. They also tend to encourage professional development.

Professional Development

The security profession changes rapidly. Innovations, such as the development of computerized guard tour systems, have changed the way guard companies do business. Economic trends, such as the substantial increase in insurance premiums in the 1970s, have had a tremendous impact on the guard industry. In a world where knowledge is power and where the use of technology can affect the winning bid, the guard company manager cannot afford to neglect professional development training.

Guard company managers have a wealth of training opportunities in professional training seminars and publications that frequently are ignored. These opportunities focus on an individual's professional development both as a manager and as a guard manager. They also provide information on new techniques and technology that may allow the company to operate more competitively.

Training usually comes through seminars and membership in professional associations. With so many security and management seminars being offered, it is important to pick only those that enhance individual professional development or meet a particular company need. The same can be said of professional organizations. Generally, if the only requirement for membership is payment of a fee, the organization is probably not worth joining for professional reasons. One organization that every guard force manager should consider joining is the American Society for Industrial Security, which is valuable for its emphasis on the professional advancement of the security industry and its access to professional resources.

The professional manager should also have a selected reading list that includes professional books and publications. There are a number of business-oriented newsletters that are useful to senior management such as the *Lipman Report* and *Security Letter.* Large national companies often subscribe to newspaper and magazine clipping services or to computer bulletin boards such as ASISNET.

It is easy, however, to overload on information. Consequently, a professional development program should have a focus and set goals. Unlike training goals for the company, however, these professional development goals should be personally developed and reflect the long-term professional goals of the manager.

10

Supervision

It is not enough for a company to set standards, although this is an important first step. Standards must be clearly communicated to workers and must be constantly reinforced. In addition, workers need strong role models who can demonstrate the company's commitment to standards and who can direct the incorporation of those standards in the worker's day-to-day activities. These role models are the supervisors who deal with the guards on a daily basis and the managers who direct the operations of the company.

Supervision takes place on many different levels. Senior and mid-level managers should make occasional visits to client sites both to discuss quality of service with the client and to inspect the guards at that site. Roving supervisors can visit several sites during their shift. On-site supervisors oversee day-to-day activities for all guards at their assigned locations. Supervision represents a continuum that reaches from the highest levels of the company down to the individual guard. It is critical that all levels communicate with each other and understand the goals and standards that they are seeking to implement.

The ranks and titles of supervisors should reflect the company's corporate philosophy. The most common system is the paramilitary rank structure consisting of sergeants, lieutenants, captains, etc. If the company has decided to project a corporate rather than a paramilitary image, titles such as site supervisor, area supervisor, site manager, etc., may be used.

Regardless of title, each supervisor must have a clear understanding of where he or she fits into the company hierarchy and of his or her duties, responsibilities, and level of authority.

Levels of Supervision

First-Line Supervisors

The first-line supervisor is the backbone of any supervisory system. He or she is the company representative with whom the guard will have the most contact. This supervisor will also have more direct contact with the client than any other member of the company. It is critical, therefore, to select the best possible supervisors, pay them accordingly, and make a commitment to provide training and support to them.

Most companies will provide for a site supervisor when bidding a large contract that involves multiple posts. However, this is not always true with smaller contracts. Every guard must have a clearly identified supervisor who has responsibility for that guard and for post operations. For the basic 1-24-7 post, the supervisor is generally the Monday-to-Friday day-shift guard. This supervisor may not necessarily be of formal supervisory rank (e.g., sergeant, group chief, site commander, etc.) but may simply be a lead or senior guard. Nevertheless, he or she should receive additional compensation for any additional supervisory work that is required.

For posts involving only a limited number of guards, the supervisor will most likely be a roving or patrol supervisor who is responsible for several client locations. This type of supervisor may also oversee the activities of the lead guards at various sites. In some companies, the position of patrol supervisor is considered an entry-level management position and includes responsibility for the management of all activities at assigned client sites.

The first-line supervisor has a number of responsibilities that revolve around the client and the guards at his or her site. The supervisor should meet daily with the client and receive any changes to the post orders, notification of special events, or concerns about service. These are then communicated to the guard company office and to the guards concerned. The supervisor also provides the client with copies of any reports that are required under the contract and briefs him or her on any significant guard activities during the reporting period.

The supervisor checks the appearance and duty performance of the guards at the site. On a 1-24-7 post, this is done by checking the guard that the supervisor relieves and the one that relieves the supervisor. Performance is checked by reviewing the post log and reports. The supervisor should periodically question the guards about post procedures and emergency actions and about company policies and procedures.

The supervisor has the onerous task of dealing with routine administrative matters pertaining to the guards. This may include review and certification of time sheets, review and submission of daily activity and incident reports, submission of requests for leave and time off, and scheduling. It may also involve the consolidation of reports and the preparation of a single exception report that summarizes post activity for the previous twenty-four hours (Figure 10.1). For this reason, the first-line supervisor must receive

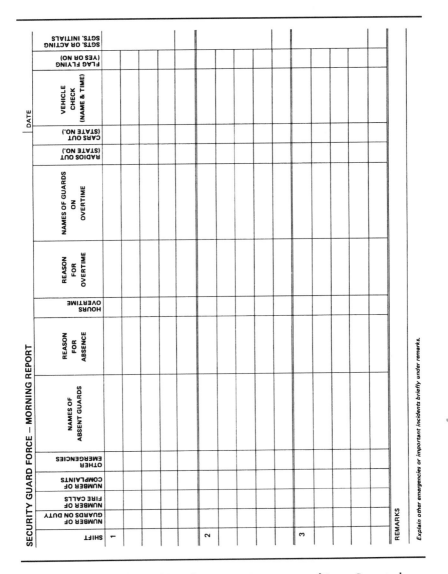

Figure 10.1 Consolidated first-line supervisory report. [From Guy et al., *Forms for Safety and Security Management*. (Boston: Butterworth Publishers, 1981.)]

specialized training in reporting and administration and be familiar with company personnel policies and procedures as they pertain to his or her duties.

An important task of the first-line supervisor is training and coaching, particularly on-the-job instruction for new guards. The attitudes and skills that the new guard acquires reflect those demonstrated by the supervisor during training. The same is true of sustainment training received by all guards at the site. The importance that the supervisor gives to this task will be clearly demonstrated by the guard's subsequent performance. The supervisor can also significantly improve a guard's performance by coaching him or her on those skills in which the guard is weak. The most common weakness found in guards is poor report writing, a task easily improved by coaching.

Second-Level Supervisors

Second-level supervisors usually are viewed as representatives of management, although they may not be actual managers. These supervisors oversee the first-line supervisors and may serve as on-site supervisors or managers at large facilities and as roving supervisors. In the paramilitary rank system, they constitute the officer ranks.

Second-level supervisors do not necessarily have day-to-day contact with the guards as do the first-line supervisors. They do, however, have a direct influence on these guards through the guidance and direction they provide to the first-line supervisors. In addition, the second-level supervisor is responsible for checking and reviewing all the reports and administrative actions processed by the first-line supervisor. The successful second-level supervisor will also conduct periodic inspections of the guards as a check on the job performance of the first-line supervisor.

The second-level supervisor performs a critical function in providing training to the first-line supervisor. Consequently, the second-level supervisor must be totally familiar with company policies and standards and must have a working knowledge of all post orders for the guards for whom he or she is responsible.

Because of his or her familiarity with company policies, the second-level supervisor can be a valuable administrative resource to the company. By training these supervisors in administrative procedures and delegating a certain amount of the administrative burden to them, it is possible to reduce the number of people required for the administrative staff. For example, rather than just consolidating the time sheets for the guards for which they are responsible, second-level supervisors can be trained to calculate the appropriate payroll data for each guard. Second-level supervisors can also be trained to conduct follow-up investigations on incidents reported by the guards.

Entry-Level Managers

Anyone who has spent any time in the guard industry has had to "pay their dues" as a new manager. The entry-level manager is usually responsible for a number of client accounts and supervises a number of second- and first-level supervisors. He or she deals with client complaints and requests for services, deals with administrative and disciplinary matters for the guards working at those sites, and may serve as scheduler, dispatcher, and payroll clerk for those accounts. The entry-level manager usually serves as the on-call manager, the first person notified after-hours of a problem or complaint at a client site.

Entry-level managers are the foundation on which guard companies rest. While the branch and corporate managers set policy and goals, it is the entry-level manager that runs the day-to-day operations of the company. This position is a high stress job, requiring a tremendous amount of overtime and on-call time. For these reasons, there is a high turnover rate among entry-level managers.

Because of the high turnover rate and the frequent need to have a newly hired manager "hit the ground running," many companies do not invest any time in training or preparing new managers for their duties. Even where training programs exist, there is a tendency to rely heavily on on-the-job training. The result is that the manager who deals directly with clients who have complaints or problems or who makes decisions on administrative or personnel issues affecting the guards is frequently the least-trained, most-inexperienced manager in the company. To avoid this situation, the guard company must devote a considerable amount of attention to the training of new managers.

Training provides the skills that the manager needs to do his or her job (see chapter 9). However, even more important is the designation of a mentor, an older, more experienced manager who provides advice and guidance to the new manager. More important, the mentor serves as a "sympathetic ear," helping to explain the reasons behind company policies and procedures and helping the new manager maintain perspective. The mentor may not necessarily be the same person who administers the management training program but should be selected for empathy and strong counseling skills.

Senior Management

The final level of supervision is senior management. In a large national company, this may include a middle to senior manager who serves as branch manager. In a small company, the owner may fulfill this function or may have delegated it to a general manager. In any event, the members of senior management do not focus on day-to-day operations at client sites. Their proper interest is in the realm of long-range planning and policy making. However, senior management must demonstrate sufficient interest in day-to-day operations to ensure that company standards are being met.

While a senior manager should not be reviewing guard reports on a daily basis, he or she should require a summary report from the operations staff each day that highlights any special activity, incidents, or problems encountered by the guards. Summary reports are easily generated through exception reporting systems and by the use of computerized guard management programs. The manager should be informed of any client complaints and of the actions taken by his or her staff to respond to the complaints.

It is critical that senior management spend time in the field checking on the quality of service being provided. This includes two basic components: inspecting guards and supervisors and talking to clients. Many guard companies require that their branch manager contact each client at least monthly. Others have a senior corporate executive periodically contact clients to verify that they are receiving quality service.

Supervisory Techniques

Conducting Inspections

A primary duty of supervisors, particularly first-line supervisors, is to inspect the guards on duty at a client's site. Unfortunately, most companies do not provide any guidelines as to what is expected. To be effective, an inspection program must be as carefully developed as any other company operation.

The basis of any inspection is the company standards that should have been issued in booklet form and explained to each guard upon hiring. As described earlier, these standards tell the guard how he or she should be uniformed, what equipment they should have, and how they should be performing their duties.

Inspections should also be based on knowledge of the post orders for the site to which the guard is assigned. To provide quality service, the guard must know what the client wants done and what is being protected at the site. The post orders also list any special equipment that should be available.

Finally, the guard should have a working knowledge of the basics of physical security, which should have formed part of the guard's preassignment training and should be reinforced in sustainment training. Subjects for inspection could include how to contact police and fire departments, patrol patterns, criminal activity indicators, and so forth.

To ensure that each inspection is impartial, the company should develop a checklist such as that shown in Figure 10.2. Once completed and signed by the guard, the inspection sheet can be placed in the guard's personnel folder.

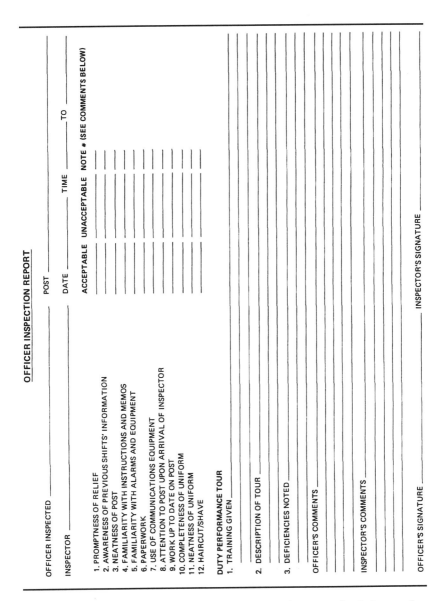

Figure 10.2 Inspection checklist. [From Guy et al., *Forms for Safety and Security Management.* (Boston: Butterworth Publishers, 1981.)]

Using manifold paper (multiple copies) allows the guard and the supervisor to each keep a copy for any follow-up inspections.

As an alternative to the inspection report, many companies use a supervisors log (Figure 10.3). This has the advantage of showing the level of activity of the supervisor and the overall status of the guard force for which he or she is responsible. It has the disadvantage of not providing for a detailed,

LOCATION	GUARDS ON DUTY	Time Inspection Covered		Client Contact?	Appearance Satisfactory?	Performing Duties Properly?	See Notes	GUARD'S SIGNATURE
		From	To					

SUPERVISORS REPORT

SUPERVISOR:_____   DATE:_____   TIME PERIOD:_____

GUARD	Details of client contacts, complaints or violations.	Action Taken or Recommendations

GUARD	Details of training or coaching provided to guard	RECOMMENDATIONS

Figure 10.3   Supervisor's log.

individual inspection that can be filed with an individual guard's records. The optimum approach is to use both, with the supervisor's log being the primary document reviewed by the operations staff.

The supervisor and guard should also make appropriate entries in the post logbook and on the daily activity report, demonstrating to the client that the guard is being supervised on a regular basis.

A proper inspection includes a visual inspection of the guard and his or her uniform; a quiz on company standards, post orders, and general security subjects; and an inventory of any assigned post property. If time permits, the supervisor should walk a tour with the guard. This allows the supervisor to re-familiarize himself or herself with the site and provides an opportunity to conduct additional training with the guard.

Disciplinary Action

To ensure that standards are enforced, supervisors must have the authority to take disciplinary action against guards who do not react to verbal warnings. However, as was pointed out in chapter 5, disciplinary measures, particularly termination, can result in legal action if not administered fairly and impartially. For this reason, a supervisor's authority over disciplinary action must be set by company policy and must be subject to review.

A supervisor generally has several disciplinary tools available. The pri-

---

EMPLOYEE MISCONDUCT NOTICE

Date_____

TO PERSONNEL DEPARTMENT:

Time
Name of Employee_____ No. _____ Dept. _____

The above-named employee has displayed the following misconduct, and has been warned that this misconduct will be entered on his Personnel Record.

MISCONDUCT (Check where applicable and specify details in section indicated below)

Smoking in Restricted Areas .... ☐	General Inefficiency......................... ☐
Leaving Work Without Permission................. ☐	a) Quality .... ☐
Violation of Safety Rules or Dept. Rules .... ☐	b) Quantity .... ☐
Refusal To Carry Out Supervisor's Instructions .... ☐	c) Accuracy .... ☐
Irregular Attendance.......................... ☐ (Specify No. of absences to date)	Discourtesy Toward Guest...................... ☐
	Discourtesy Toward Fellow Employee............. ☐
Frequent Tardiness........................... ☐	(Mention other Employee)
Violation of Eating Regulations .... ☐	Attitude................................. ☐
Breakage .... ☐	Carelessness .... ☐
Poor Service .... ☐	Other................................. ☐

Specify Misconduct in Detail _____
_____
_____
_____

EMPLOYEE COMMENTS _____
_____
_____
_____

DISCIPLINARY ACTION TAKEN _____

　　　　(REPRIMAND)　　(LAYOFF)　　(OTHER)

SIGNATURE OF SUPERVISOR

I acknowledge receipt of this notice

ORIGINAL (WHITE) TO EMPLOYEE
DUPLICATE (BLUE) TO PERSONNEL DEPT.
TRIPLICATE (PINK) TO DEPARTMENT HEAD
QUADRUPLICATE (YELLOW) TO UNION

_____
SIGNATURE OF EMPLOYEE

Figure 10.4　Written warning. [From Guy et al., *Forms for Safety and Security Management*. (Boston: Butterworth Publishers, 1981.)]

mary corrective action is a verbal warning. Should the guard repeat the offense or if it is of such a nature that a verbal warning is inappropriate, the supervisor can issue a written warning, a copy of which is forwarded to management for review (Figure 10.4). Depending on the offense, management may choose to exercise any of the options discussed in chapter 5, including suspension or termination.

There are occasions, however, when the supervisor must go beyond a verbal or written warning. Examples of these types of cases are when the guard is under the influence of drugs or alcohol, out of uniform, or otherwise unfit for duty. The supervisor must have the authority to immediately relieve the guard from duty in such cases. This authority must be clearly spelled out in company policies. Note that the supervisor relieves the guard and does not terminate him or her. It is essential that all terminations be done by the personnel department after a careful review of the facts surrounding the offense.

On-Call Manager

A supervisor's authority is limited and defined by company policy. There will be times when the supervisor will encounter problems or incidents beyond the scope of his or her authority or which require a policy decision from the management team. For this reason, the supervisor should be backed up by an on-call manager.

Depending on the authority of the supervisor and the way the company is organized, the job of the on-call manager can be relatively easy or highly stressful. If the company has a twenty-four-hour dispatcher, routine problems, such as no-shows, late arrivals, and call-offs due to illness, can be dealt with at the supervisory level without the manager being involved. These routine events can be noted in the dispatcher's log. If a supervisor has the authority to relieve an unfit guard and call in a suitable replacement, this too can be handled without permission from the on-call manager. In such a case, the supervisor can either contact the manager to advise him or her of what has happened or can make a note in the supervisor's log. In such cases, the on-call manager is only contacted for serious emergencies or incidents. Because of the low incidence of calls, it is possible to designate an on-call manager for a period of up to a week.

On the other hand, if the company chooses to withhold authority from the supervisor and to hold down overhead by using an answering service after hours, the on-call manager can expect to field numerous routine calls throughout his or her duty period. If this is the case, the on-call duty should be rotated daily among the management team.

The on-call manager needs several tools with which to work. The first is a reliable means of being contacted. Requiring an on-call manager to remain by his or her phone or to periodically check in with a dispatcher or answering service is unrealistic and unnecessary in this age of cellular phones and miniature pagers. At a minimum, the on-call person should be equipped with a pager. If the company uses FM radios, one can also be issued to the manager, but this should be a backup means of contact.

The manager will also need a copy of the weekly schedule, a roster of available guards, and an up-to-date telephone directory that includes emergency client contact numbers. Finally, the manager will need any appropriate forms and logs required by company policy.

Quality Control

Supervision in the guard company has a single focus: the control of quality of service delivered to the client. As was mentioned in chapter 4, guards fulfill an extremely important role in the marketing of services. The level of service provided by the guards has a direct bearing on the retention of guard contracts and can indirectly influence potential clients. People tend to forget good service quickly but have a very long memory for bad service.

Supervisory staff, therefore, function as a check on the level of service being provided to the client. Supervisors evaluate how well service is being provided and how it might be improved. They identify problems and solve them before they escalate. Where there has been a failure of service, supervisors perform the function of damage control—swiftly investigating and dealing with the issue and assuring clients that failures of service are anomalies in the company, not the norm.

Most important, supervisors set examples for the guards. A supervisor with a bad attitude toward the company or the client will have a negative impact on the performance of the guards he or she supervises. A supervisor who is too lazy or too timid to inspect and correct a guard's uniform or performance will gradually degrade the quality of service at those posts for which he or she is responsible.

A sound quality control program rests on the strengths of the supervisory staff. It requires careful inspection of service and the immediate correction of deficiencies. It requires regular contact with clients and attention to client complaints. Supervisors must be proactive in identifying these problems and must be responsive to client complaints. Each level of supervision must be supportive of other levels and of this single goal: the delivery of quality service in order to retain clients.

References

Arscott, Robert D., Marc P. Lambert, and Sharon W. Revis. "Choosing and Using Contract Security." *Security Management,* June 1991.

Astor, Saul D. *Loss Prevention: Controls and Concepts.* Boston: Butterworth Publishers, 1978.

ATA, Inc. *Guard Contract Kit: A Guide to Cost-Effective Security Guard Contract Negotiations.* Fredericktown, Ohio: ATA, Inc., 1993.

Barefoot, J. Kirk, and David A. Maxwell. *Corporate Security Administration and Management.* Boston: Butterworth Publishers, 1987.

Beaudette, John. "Hiring: Caveat Employer." *Security Management,* April 1992.

Behar, Richard, "Thugs in Uniform," *Time,* 9 March 1992.

Byrne, Brendan T., chairman, National Advisory Committee on Criminal Justice Standards and Goals. *Private Security: Report of the Task Force on Private Security.* Washington, D.C.: Government Printing Office, 1976.

Caine, Bruce, "Role Making and the Assumption of Leadership." In *A Study of Organizational Leadership,* ed. United States Military Academy Office of Military Leadership. Harrisburg, Pa.: Stackpole Books, 1976.

Carlyon, Scott M. "A Class Act." *Security Management,* May 1991.

Chernicoff, Joseph L. "Contract Guards Coping with Technology." *Access Control,* September 1991.

Chernicoff, Joseph L. "Roles, Demands Change for Contract Guards." *Access Control*, March 1991.

Cunningham, W.C., and T.H. Taylor. *The Hallcrest Report: Private Security and Police in America.* Portland, Oreg.: Chancellor Press, 1984.

Dale, Ernest, and Lyndall Urwick. *Staff in Organization.* New York: McGraw-Hill, 1960.

Dalton, Dennis R. *Managing Contract Security Services: A Business Approach.* Fremont, Calif.: Mill Creek Publishing, 1991.

———. "Industry Needs Quality Standards for Guards." *Access Control*, May 1992.

———. "Contract Labor: The True Story." *Security Management*, January 1993.

Drucker, Peter F. *Management: Tasks, Responsibilities, Practices.* New York: Harper & Row, 1974.

Elig, Gene P. "Florida Takes Unprecedented Action." *Security Concepts*, November 1993.

Feliton, John R., and David B. Owen. "Guarding Against Liability." *Security Management*, September 1994.

Gallery, Shari Mendelson. *Security Training: Readings from "Security Management" Magazine.* Boston: Butterworth Publishers, 1990.

Greene, Mark R. *Insurance and Risk Management for Small Business.* Washington, D.C.: United States Small Business Administration, 1981.

Guy, Edward T., John J. Merrigan, Jr., and John A. Wanat. *Forms for Safety and Security Management.* Boston: Butterworth Publishers, 1981.

———. *Supervisory Techniques for the Security Professional.* Boston: Butterworth Publishers, 1981.

Hamit, Francis. "Perpetuating the Rent-a-Cop Myth." *Security Management*, June 1991.

Healy, Richard J., and Timothy J. Walsh. *Principles of Security Management.* Long Beach, Calif.: Professional Publications, 1983.

Ingber, Clifford J. "A Duty to Protect." *Security Management*, December 1993.

Jackson, William E. "Effective Guard Training Must be Ongoing." *Access Control*, July 1993.

Jenkins, C. Gordon. "How to Find 1/10th of an Employee." *Security Management*, August 1987.

Jones, John W. "Trends and Issues: Integrity Tests." *Security*, October 1991.

Keeling, B. Lewis, Norman F. Kallaus, and John J. W. Neuner. *Administrative Office Management*. Cincinnati, Ohio: South-Western Publishing Co., 1978.

King, Carl E., and Dain Dunston. "The Proof's on the Paper." *Security Management*, January 1992.

Lang, William G. "Should Training Be Performance Based?" *Security Management*, November 1994.

Ledvinka, J., and V.G. Scarpello. *Federal Regulation of Personnel and Human Resource Management*. Boston: PWS-Kent, 1991.

Levinson, Jay C. *Guerrilla Marketing: Secrets for Making Big Profits from Your Small Business*. Boston: Houghton Mifflin Company, 1984.

Mancebo, Marty. "Selecting a Test to Get the Best." *Security Management*, January 1992.

Marquis, Lisa. "Times—They Are A-changing: Private Security Patrols Cut Crime in Times Square." *Security*, August 1994.

Minion, Ronald R. "Bootstrap Training Builds Quality." *Security*, December 1990.

Muntz, Alan M. "Contracting for the Right Relationship." *Security Management*, June 1991.

National Advisory Committee on Criminal Justice Standards and Goals. *Private Security: Report of the Task Force on Private Security*. Washington, D.C.: U.S. Government Printing Office, 1976.

Pederson, Dwight S. "Computerizing Contract Security." *Security Management*, December 1993.

Peters, Thomas J., and Robert H. Waterman, Jr. *In Search of Excellence: Lessons from America's Best-Run Companies*. New York: Harper & Row, 1982.

Ramsey, Jackson E., and Inez L. Ramsey. *Budgeting Basics: How to Survive the Budgeting Process*. New York: Franklin Watts, 1985.

Rockwell, Robert R. *Business Management Practices for the Contract Security Guard Operator*. Walnut Creek, Calif.: Robert R. Rockwell Consulting Services, 1987.

Rosen, Mark B. "Trust But Verify: A Good Contract Security Agreement Protects Both Vendor and Client." *Security Management*, November 1992.

Roughton, James E. "Deciphering the Fine Print: Guidelines for Selecting Quality Contract Security." *Security Management*, November 1992.

Russell, Rebecca D. "Office Training: Identify Your Options." *Security,* May 1990.

———. "Uniform Dress." *Security,* June 1991.

Schnabolk, Charles. *Physical Security: Practices and Technology.* Boston: Butterworth Publishers, 1983.

Sennewald, Charles A. *Effective Security Management.* Boston: Butterworth Publishers, 1978.

Snodgrass, Tod. *Office Purchasing Guide.* Torrance, Calif.: Lowen Publishing, 1986.

Sullivan, Craig A. "Tactical Sleeping." *Police,* June 1991.

Sweet, Donald H. *A Manager's Guide to Conducting Terminations.* Lexington, Mass.: Lexington Books, 1989.

Taylor, Frederick W. *Scientific Management.* New York: Harper & Brothers, 1947.

Tyska, Louis A., and Lawrence J. Fennelly and Associates. *Security in the Year 2000 and Beyond.* New York: ETC, 1987.

Vassel, William C., Edward A. Ramsdell, and David O. Tharp. "Bringing Contract Services On-Line." *Security Management,* December 1993.

Villarreal, Carlos. "A Triumphant Tale of Training." *Security Management,* November 1994.

Virga, Patricia H., ed. *The NMA Handbook for Managers.* Englewood Cliffs, N.J.: Prentice Hall, Inc., 1987.

Walsh, Timothy J., and Richard J. Healy. *Protection of Assets Manual.* Santa Monica, Calif.: The Merrit Company, 1987.

Wathen, Thomas W. "Increasing Threats Change Role of Guard." *Access Control,* May 1993.

Zalud, Bill. "Better Scheduling—Save Time, Money." *Security,* March 1988.

Index